ART OF THE LOWER GANGES VALLEY:
A PICTORIAL MONOGRAPH

ART OF THE LOWER GANGES VALLEY: A PICTORIAL MONOGRAPH

Prasanta Kumar Mandal

AGAM KALA PRAKASHAN
DELHI

First Published 2013

Photographs: Mr.Tapas Kumar Maiti

ISBN : 978-81-7320-135-6

Published by:
Dr. Agam Prasad, M.A., Ph.D., Diploma in Museology
For Agam Kala Prakashan
34, Central Market, Ashok Vihar
Delhi - 110 052
Tel.: 011-27212195, 65688806-7
Fax: 91-11-27212195
Email: agambooks@gmail.com, agambook@yahoo.com
www.agamkala.com

Composed by:
Aman Printographics
Delhi - 110 052
Mobile: 9891395309

Printed by:
Chawla Offsets
Delhi-110 052

Printed in India

To
My Mother

CONTENTS

PREFACE

After the publication of my previous monograph, titled, 'Art and Artifacts of Bone and Antler in the Lower Ganges Valley', in the year 1993, I thought it necessary to bring out a volume on the art in bone and antler, in order to highlight different aspects of this prehistoric plastic art. I have tried to deal with the forms, styles and social significance of the objects concerned as far as practicable with available resources. A considerable number of photographs have been included in the present monograph for an understanding and appreciation of our readers.

I am aware of the fact that, really it is hard to do justice to our materials which are so new, unique and ancient – especially when no other site in the sub-continent has yielded so far such kind of objects either through excavation or surface collection. In spite of that, I think, the importance of these things cannot be denied and so I have ventured to bring out the presentation in an anticipation of future discovery in the country and the proper evaluation of such kind of art in the socio-cultural matrix of Indian prehistory, as a whole.

In this connection I would take the opportunity to express my gratitude to my 'guru', the late Dr. Tarasish Mukhopadhyay, an anthropologist. I am grateful to my friends, Dr. Kamal Kumar Kundu and Mr.Tapas Kumar Maiti for their suggestions and help all along for its total improvement. Really it is difficult to convince anyone about prehistoric art by the descriptions only – especially when its forms, styles and contents etc., are quite new and unfamiliar. Photographs of the examples of art are essential in this regard. I was quite helpless. At this juncture, Mr.Tapas Kumar Maiti realized my situation and took upon himself the difficult task of taking photographs. He photographed all specimens and did everything from start to finish with utmost care and interest. He personally incurred much expenditure for this purpose even. Half the credit of this monograph is his. I salute him. I am also grateful to the members of his family who helped a lot during whole period. I am indebted to Mr. Sajal Kumar Gantait and Mrs. Pratima Gantait who nursed me when I was confined to bed after a serious bus accident for long 3 months during which period the manuscript of this monograph was written. In fine, I like to express my indebtedness to my wife Smt. Chhanda Mandal, son Dr. Koushik Mandal and daughter Joyita Mandal who have always stood by me and inspired me for the publication of the present monograph.

Prasanta Kumar Mandal

PART - I

SURVEY AND INTERPRETATIOCN OF THE ART IN BONES AND ANTLERS

Prehistoric man made tools for use in the home, weapons for hunting and works of art for social obligations. All these things taken together are known by a common name, artifact. Artifacts were made of stone, bone and wood, etc. For the purpose of the present monograph, we would deal with those artifacts that were made by using art in the mediums of bone and antler only. In my previous volume, titled, 'Art and Artifacts of Bone and Antler in the Lower Ganges Valley', the artifacts of all kinds of bone and antler were dealt with. In course of explorations along the sloping right bank of the Rupnarayan, a number of prehistoric sites were discovered and the above artifacts were collected together with other antiquities from a single site of Natshal (N 22.20672 ; E 088.02864), near the river's confluence with the Hooghly, in Tamluk subdivision in the district of Purba Medinipur, West Bengal. Now the site is under the jurisdiction of Haldia subdivision. It may be further mentioned that, as the examples were not stratified and were collected as surface finds, their exact dating was difficult. But in consideration of absence of these kinds of objects in Indian archaeology of historical periods, they were thought to belong to prehistoric period and the said presentation was brought out with the description of some significant tools, weapons and works of art along with their photographs to avoid misconception and facilitate to our readers to have an overall idea about the kinds of objects and their probable assemblage.

The site of Natshal yielded varied archaeological objects that comprise the following:

1. human mandibles, femur, and clavicle;
2. large and pigmy tools of fossilized and partly fossilized bones, teeth and antlers,like: hammers, points, scrapers, blades, gravers, awls, knives, chisels, barbs and bone harpoons, etc., and a few microliths;
3. Neolithic celts and polished bone tools;
4. varied works of art on bone and antler; two examples in stone;
5. beads of clay, animal teeth, metal, precious and semi-precious stones;
6. pottery, like: hand-made pottery, black burnished ware, black and red ware, degenerated N.B.P. ware, rouletted ware and those of other kinds of early historical and mediaeval periods;
7. terracotta plaques most of which betray the Gupta style of art;
8. a few stone images of about 8th – 9th centuries;
9. copper cast coins – both square and round of early historical periods;
10. terracotta sealing bearing inscriptions; and
11. grinding stones, dabbers and terracotta sling balls.

Presence of all above kinds of objects at a single site signifies the fact that here human habitation continued over hundreds upon hundreds of years from prehistoric times to the present day. The following points may be considered crucial for an understanding of the importance of the artifacts of bone and antler collected from the concerned site:

1. presence of large number of tools of fossil bone and antler, together with varied types of absurdly diminutive tools of the same materials - the latter types seemingly

sharing a common concern with microliths in respect of their shapes, sizes and functional use;
2. engravings, carvings, paintings and clay modellings on bones and antlers as examples of works of art;
3. co-existence of such tools and works of art at a particular site;
4. forms, styles and medium of art being indicative of 'home or mobile art';
5. presence of bone harpoons; and finally,
6. discovery of fossilized human skeletal remains from the same site.

In the context of what has been stated above, here in the present monograph our purpose would be to interpret the artifacts that include the works of art only. As neither among the craftsmen of this region today, nor in any cultural assemblage, known from the spades of archaeologists in India, do we come across the kind of works of art we are going to deal with, we are inclined to consider them as examples of prehistoric art, until such stratified objects of historical periods are available to refute our hypothesis. Now as our works of art are in bone and antler and we consider them to be ascribable to the prehistoric period, it would be worthwhile to try to understand, in the light of the available literature, how – when – where and to what extent these mediums came to have been utilized as such first and then in that perspective to attempt to embark upon our proposed purpose of interpretation.

Bone and antler have rarely been used as medium of art throughout the course of historical periods. But, they are seen to have been used to make tools since the early days of prehistory, as pointed out by Raymond Dart for the first time in 1949 and he called it osteodontokeratic culture ('bone-tooth-antler-culture'), basing his hypothesis upon the study of 'split bones and teeth belonging to Australopithecines from sites in South Africa', (Jelinek, 1975 : 122). These things as medium of art came to have been used largely since the Upper Palaeolithic times and certainly quite logically man began using them for creation of art from earlier periods in the forms of engraving, drawing and painting, sculpture and modelling. Side by side, regarding prevalence of art before, L.S.B. Leakey says, "a few rare examples of drawings made with finger - tips on wet clay, on the ceilings and walls of a few caves ... serve to fortify our belief that art in these forms must have been fairly common before painting and engraving were thought of." (1953 : 147).

However, examples of prehistoric art, i.e., 'home or mobile art' and 'cave or parietal art' are "discovered from many sites, stretching eastwards from France and Spain to the Russian Urals. Forms, styles, regional divergences of magico-religious or utilitarian significance, aesthetic ideal, problems of dating and interpretations etc., of prehistoric art have been dealt with in the works of Burkitt (1929), Adam (1949), Leakey (1953), Christensen (1960) Prufer (1966), Jelinek (1975), Waechter (1976) and others." (Mandal, 1993 : 18).

In excavations, the Upper Palaeolithic home sites near caves have yielded innumerable bones portions of which are seen to have been shaped in the form of animal heads or their surfaces are found to have been covered with different motifs. But very few of such bones have been reported from home sites in open stations of Upper Palaeotlithic date. In this context, Burkitt makes a significant comment, "Theoretically there is no reason why examples of the home art should not also be found in open stations of Upper Palaeolithic date. Indeed, engravings have been brought forward, but unfortunately in every case so far there has been, for various reasons, an element of doubt as to the authenticity or the true age of the specimen. In the nature of the case it would be hardly likely that such fragile objects as decorated bones, etc., would often survive the rough and tumble and mechanical weathering to which industries from open stations are almost invariably exposed. (1962 : 137)"

It is now held that Lower Palaeolithic man made bone tools, but proof of such artifacts has been available since the Mousterian culture of the Neanderthal race. Besides stone, cave walls, etc., men of the Upper Palaeolithic cultures, comprising the Aurignacian, the Solutrean and the Magdalenian – all having been known after the place names, like : Aurignac, Solutre and La Madeleine of France, exploited bone, antler and ivory extensively for creating art. Art was of different forms and styles depicting various motifs with varying degrees of perfection that was at its best in the Magdalenian. Other than the beautiful naturalistic representations of beings and geometric patterns, suggestion pictures and conventionalised presentation of beings came to be depicted. Here it may be noted that representation of man was comparatively rare during the period. Different subjects were engraved, carved and painted on bone and antler. Tools and weapons were decorated with beautiful engravings and carvings. What made its emergence in the Aurignecian, with a decline in the Solutrean reached the zenith of excellence in the Magdalenian followed by its sad decline and decay towards the end of the Upper Palaeolithic culture.

'In India, we have come across only cave art so far. In 1880, it was first discovered near Mirzapur by Archibald Carlleyle and J. Cockburn. Since then many other cave paintings have been found and variously dated. While some scholars prefer an Upper Palaeolithic date for some of the paintings, others do not like for them a date beyond the fifth century B.C., at the earliest. However, on the basis of 'Style, context, superimposition and general indications of antiquity' the rock art of central and peninsular India covers a considerable period of time (Brown : 1947 ; Adam : 1949 ; Piggot : 1950 ; Gordon : 1960 ; Bridget and Allchin : 1968).'

In this context, it may be noted that, stratigraphical evidences have been reported from Bihar, Uttar Pradesh, West Bengal, Madhya Pradesh, and Maharashtra, Andhra, Mysore and Tamil Nadu to place the blade and burin industries in a period between Middle Palaeolithic and Mesolithic. The blades and burins from Chittoor and Kurnool are similar to the classic examples of the Upper Palaeolithic cultures of Western Europe and West Asia. In this context, Sankalia states, "there is little doubt that the industry does belong to the closing phase of the formation of river deposits, particularly all over peninsular India. And there is also palaeontological evidence from the Billasurgam caves to place this phase in the Upper Pleistocene. But what is still missing is the associated art work in bone, antler and ivory, paintings and engravings on bone and soft stone and above all, the remains of Homo Sapiens himself, who in all probability was the creator of all this varied work. Both the latter cannot be expected in open river sites. (1974 : 209)"

However, discovery of artifacts of bone and antler from an open river site of Natshal is extremely important and meaningful. Natshal is not within the fossil bearing zone and as such it may not be denied that the raw materials for making these artifacts were carried probably from somewhere of the hilly regions lying in the eastern part of Chotanagpur Plateau and its adjacent areas and the specimens bearing the works of art of our study, which are mostly fossilized or are in a state of mineralization, we believe, survived 'the rough and tumble and mechanical weathering' which they were expected to have been exposed to over thousands of years.

It seems relevant to discuss about some of the near-by sites. In course of explorations the present writer discovered a number of prehistoric sites along the right bank of the Rupnarayan lying to the north of Natshal and to the south of the present-day Tamluk which is identified with the ancient city-port of Tamralipta. The sites are: Ichhapur, Bar Amirtberia, and Kumbhachak Natshal. Besides other antiquities of early historical periods, the said sites have yielded a few microliths, many bone points, fish-hook, Neolithic celts, painted grey ware, ordinary and painted black-and-red ware, red ware and objects of copper including a copper celt. A unilaterally two-barbed bone harpoon has been collected from Tamluk, which has been dated in the 2nd millennium B.C. by Mr. B. K. Thaper, an archaeologist. On the left bank of the Hooghly and further south of Natshal similar finds were recorded by the present writer in Deulpota near Diamond Harbour in 24 Parganas district, where Upper Palaeolithic stone tools (Das Gupta, 1964: 48) and stone tools of Middle Stone Age (Sankalia, 1974: 51) have been found. On the basis of the above finds, it may be said that this area in the lower Ganges valley was well populated since the 2nd millennium, B. C., at least.

Again, in Kumbhachak Natshal, present writer collected a large lower jaw of a bovine animal. The teeth were removed and the jaw was made smooth so that microliths or similar kinds of small tools of fossil bones could be fixed to make a sickle. This suggestion was also supported by the Late Mr. Pares Chandra Das Gupta, the then Director of Archaeology,Government of West Bengal.

In this background, if we turn to Natshal, we note with surprise that, Natshal, in particular, yields altogether different types of tools--large and small, of fossil and mineralized bones and antlers. Among larger types we find scrapers, points, awls, blades and harpoons. Flaking is noticeable on a number of tools. Many burin-like tools occur. This site abounds in small tools that have parallels in microlithic industries. Here we would specially mention two small bone tools that are made in exact similarity of animal teeth and no doubt, they were used as sickle-blades. If one looks at the entire repertoire of tools of Natshal, one would be taken aback to note their similarity with their lithic counterpart. Again some tools are totally innovative of the bone industry. These tools are particularly peculiar for their sharp semicircular cutting edge at one end with a notch. However, it appears that one would not be wrong if he infers that, the people making these bone tools had intimacy with those who made stone tools and lived afar where stone was available, or else the former group used to come here with bundles of bones and nodules of fine grained stone to make tools, for hunting, fishing and agriculture seasonally and finally settled here. They created art in bone and antler. Two examples of art in stone have also been collected from Natshal.

For the convenience of analysis, some traits of 130 examples of art have been recorded in a table. Selected traits or features include: measurement, medium, place of occurrence of motifs on the object, motifs, forms or techniques and styles or postures. After putting scores of different traits of those examples in the table we arrive at the following results. It may be mentioned that we have counted twice the scores of some of the traits of seven examples, excluding those, like measurement, medium, etc., as depictions occur on two sides of the same specimen.

Summary of the scores of the said table is shown in Table No. 1, titled, 'FINAL SCORE-SHEET SHOWING DIFFERENT TRAITS OF WORKS OF ART OF BONE AND ANTLER, and on the basis of the same table we arrive at Table No. 2, titled, 'FLUCTUATIONS OF EXAMPLES OF ART IN RESPECT OF LENGTH AND BREADTH', in order to form an idea regarding the space available for depiction of motifs.

We may now attempt trait-wise discussion one by one. First of all- measurement. By putting the measurements (in cms) of length and breadth of all specimens in the table, we are in a position to state that, the length of most of the specimens ranges from 3 – 10 cms and the breadth from 2 – 6 cms. In taking the measurements decimal has been avoided and it is counted to the next higher integer. Again from 16 specimens, we notice that the bones and antlers bearing depiction range from 4 – 14 cms in length. In case of 3 bone discs, diameter reads 6 and 9 cms. We have taken measurements of length and breadth of broken discs and of those that have no uniform diameter. However, from the above table we may understand that, the artists preferred mostly the specimens that were 3 – 10 cms in length and 2 – 6 cms in breadth. They had to confine themselves within that short space to translate their artistic creativity. Here, it may be noted that, the artists using wood and stone and the walls of caves, etc., in the past enjoyed much freedom in this regard. They could let their artistic ingenuity play according to their sweet will. Enough space at hand and the motifs, no matter how many of them the artists chose, might be placed vertically or horizontally and the measurements of motifs varied largely. In spite of that, superposition of motifs occurred. Moreover, carving largely bases upon the thickness of the mediums and in case of wood and stone, it is enough. All kinds of relief may be well created in those mediums. But the artists had less freedom in bone in this respect. Of course, they had the opportunity to exploit the curvature of bones and peculiar formation of epiphyses – that sometimes gave the effect of relief and at times the epiphyses offered scope to give the outline of a head of a being with a little of engraved lines. However, it is evident that, the artist was skillful enough as to arrange and accommodate his motifs in that short space and to take the advantage of the natural contour of the surface of the concerned medium.

Next, comes the medium of art that consists of bone and antler. Excavation reports and the literature on prehistory are silent about the availability of works of art in these mediums in Indian archaeology. But from the site of Natshal, we have collected such examples of works of art of these mediums that remind us of the kind of art available from the caves and open air sites of alien countries. Of the 130 examples, bone specimens number 118 (90.8%) and antlers are 12 (9.2%).

Before portrayal of motifs, the selected bones and antlers were cut and split according to requirement – especially the antlers and the thick circular bone discs were cut. The round long bones were split longitudinally with pointed tools. Portrayal is seen to occur on the dorsal side of split bones generally, but the ventral side is also utilised for the purpose. What is most surprising and interesting is the carving of figures on the thick section between the dorsal and the ventral sides of bones. Out of 130 specimens, 68 examples (52.3%) bear motifs on the dorsal sides, 13(10%) on the ventral sides and on the thick section 5 (3.8%) instances are there. Long flat and round bones and antlers numbering 28 (21.5%) are utilized for the purpose. 12(9.2%) separated flat segments are seen to bear engraving, painting or modelling with clay. Thick circular discs some of which are broken mainly bear paintings and engravings. These are 11 in number that constitute 8.4% of the specimens we are concerned with.

Now about motifs. Motifs consist of human figures, animal figures, aquatic beings, strange beings and some designs and patterns. Of 70 human figures, 21 (16.1%) seem to represent male, 8 (6.1%) female and 41 (31.5%) are difficult to understand. Examples bearing animal figures are 56 in number constituting 43% of the concerned specimens. Others bearing patterns, etc., are 11. Certainly the artist had the preference for portrayal of human beings (53.7%) to the animal (43%).

On examination of the concerned examples regarding technique of depiction, it is revealed that the artist engraved and pecked, the artist carved, the artist modelled with clay in appliqué and the artist ground, painted and polished. Of all techniques engraving was the most favourite. The artist engraved motifs on all types of the aforesaid bones and antlers. Sometimes the engraving was deep and at times it was mere a scratch. 56.1% of specimens bear engravings, while carving is seen on 44.6%. Engravings and carvings were employed to portray motifs separately. But again both the techniques were employed simultaneously to depict a motif. Pecking is seen on 9 specimens together with engravings. Whether pecking was to add to beauty or to signify ailments like pox, it is hard to guess. But it is a fact that pecking has been noticed on the examples of art from Africa, as is known form literature. Two very thin pieces of bone, finely cut in the form of faces – one frontally and the other in profile are like silhouette figures. While the former specimen shows on it the cut – mark for nose, pin-holes for eyes and the painting for mouth, the latter in profile to left shows the beautifully carved lips and this possibly represents a female face.

Well levigated sticky grey clay has been used for portrayal of motifs. On the plain surface of bone, clay is used to portray eyes, nose and mouth; a broad line of white clay outlines a human head in profile to left on the flat oblong segment of bone painted in black ; a flat piece of bone cut in the shape of human head in profile to right bears clay in appliqué pasted along the border to show the forehead, nose and mouth; a thin layer of well-levigated clay on a segment of bone has been used as background and on it are engraved two faces – one a male on right kissing the mouth of a female on left, which probably represents coitus. In some instances it is seen that after small engravings and painting on bones, clay has been used. We have 8 examples in a total of 130 specimens. After engraving and carving, painting forms the largest group representing 23.8%. The surface of a specimen was made smooth by grinding, small marks of scratches are seen on the said surface. The specimen was finally painted and polished with some water repellant substance. However, painting was not always followed by polishing. Red, black and creamy red colour are seen to have been used.

Ancient artists knew the technique of presenting the figures in profile or side-view. They were apt to do it in frontal view also. Presentation of profile is especially done by engraving, painting and clay modelling and most of the examples showing frontal view are executed by carving. While 103 figures are depicted in profile, 28 are found to have been presented frontally. Again, heads or faces of human beings and animals were preferred and the artists seem to have been at ease in the art of depicting them. We have 106 examples in this regard. Presentation of the whole body is not rare. Probably an aquatic being having red bands on its body and a black circular dot for an eye, a running horned bovine animal and an animal turning its head back to its hinder part are some of the instances of presentation of full figures. We have 21 examples of this kind and it may be mentioned here that we have no problem in taking the depiction for the whole body – though all limbs, like : hands, legs and ears, etc., are absent.

Sometimes, the figures concerned suggest their standing or lying postures and the examples of this kind number 9 and 8 respectively.

In a nutshell, the matter stands as follows:

The smallest and the largest specimens measure 2.2 x .8 cms and 14 x 11 cms respectively. The examples mostly vary from 3 to 10 cms in length and from 2 to 6 cms in breadth. Bone specimens are 90.8%. 79% of split bones bear depiction on dorsal side. Depicted human and animal figures are 53.7% and 43% respectively. Depiction of motifs in profile is 79.2%, whereas that in frontal view is 21.5%. Again, while only head represents 81.5% of depiction, that of torso and the suggested whole body rests at 16.1% only. As regards technique of depiction, we notice engravings on 56.1% specimens, carving on 44.6% specimens and paintings on 23.8% specimens. However, the above fluctuations of traits would, we believe help understand the actual state of affairs and highlight the limitations, constraints as well as the attitude of the artists towards art, as a whole. The concerned artists aptly managed the entire situation and were successful in creating a sense of movement in the depicted subject. We find this phenomenon in the paintings, engravings, cravings and clay-modellings. It is expressed by way of arranging the limbs differently and showing the curve outlines of the body so as to give us the impression of movement. In the painted examples we find: an animal running, a bovine animal turning its head back reaching its hip, a reclining beast turning its head and looking back, and a bull with its curve elongated outlines of the body in an attitude to move, et cetera. In a very low bas-relief on clay is engraved a taller human male figure covering with his mouth the forepart of the face of his sexual partner. An engraved fabulous creature is seen devouring a human head. The carved and the engraved human and animal heads and figures depicted at different angles impress upon the viewer a sense of movement and it is , no doubt, a great achievement on the part of the artists concerned, that lends charm and beauty to the works of art.

Here it may be noted that, some of the physical characteristic features of different racial groups are noticeable in the depictions of human heads by the artists. From it, the anthropologists may try to provide us with an overall presumptive picture of the racial stocks which our ancestors frequenting this region belonged to. The depictions show: long head, round head, flat nose, short nose, long nose, prominent eye-brow, thick lips, heavy jaw, broad cheeks, narrow cheek, prominent cheek-bone, prominent chin, broad forehead, and long forehead receding backward. Round eyes in most cases probably represent eye sockets. However, it appears that the artist came in contact with or saw people of different racial groups and depicted their faces in art. Whatever may be the date of their depiction, it was done after the artist had come in contact with the different members of a society of a mixed population.

In this connection, in order to understand and get down to the thematic implication of the depiction of art under study, we quote views of some authorities on the following terms that seem relevant for our purpose.

Art: Regarding art, writes Herbert Read (1949: 16, 53 – 54, 62),"...art is most simply and most usually defined as an attempt to create pleasing forms. "About prehistoric art he says, "the purpose is rather to represent the most expressive aspect of each element in an object – the side view of the foot...being combined with the front view of the eyes ... the art of these primitive peoples is not naturalistic...The details of natural forms are rejected or distorted in order to suggest the prime significance of the object represented...Palaeolithic art shows a definite development from a linear or two – dimensional mode of representation in the Aurignacian period to a plastic or three – dimensional mode in the Magdalenian period ; but in the Neolithic period this plastic sensibility disappears."

Again, regarding interdependence of art and religion he goes on to say, "We look back into the past and see art and religion emerging hand in hand from the dim recess of pre-history ...

The magicians and priests of religion are identical with the creative artists, and art only exists as a function of worship or propitiation."

Religion: "Religion... consists mainly in an attitude of mind, which is largely emotional, towards man's environment in its various aspects physical, social and psychical. This expresses itself by means of actions, objects, and words. Typically there is a belief in supernatural agencies or beings who may have to be propitiated, or occasionally cajoled or threatened."

Magic: "Magic... typically a method by which the desired aim is achieved by the direct action of rites, objects, or words."

"Although... religion and magic are very distinct, yet frequently, it will be found that they merge into each other. For this reason it has been customary of late to use the term magico-religious to cover both magical and religious beliefs and practices, ..." Again, "... ritual tends to be present where the elements of chance and danger occur, but is likely to be absent when the pursuit is certain, reliable and well under the control of rational methods and technological processes."

Rite: "A customary practice of a magico-religious character ... The rite may consist of a number of ritual acts."

Sacred: "Sacred may be used of all persons, things, or actions set apart for magico-religious reasons from the profane or secular."

Sacrifice: "Any rite of consecration by which something is removed from secular use and devoted to a sacred use, this, as in the case of the blood sacrifice, often involving its destruction."

(Notes and Queries on Anthropology,
By A Committee of Section H : 1929)

Creation of art dates from the early days of human civilization. The purpose of such creation was many. It might have been to communicate what the artist thought, to others, or to win over the evil influence, or to increase fertility, or to tie-up some injured animal or to have success in hunting or to simply enjoy the beauty of his creation and so on. Art acts as a mirror of a society. It is as true at present as it had been in the past. On the basis of thematic implication of the depictions of works of art, we may now try to visualise fragmentary glimpses of what happened in the then society of this region in the past.

Now, we may pause and think and have a look at the examples. The score-sheet reveals that, depiction of heads of human and animal beings rests at 81.5%. Why so much of depiction of heads only? What prompted the artist to discard depiction of the whole body? What was the guiding impulse for such creation? A host of such queries come up to answer after such a huge lapse of time - which is a difficult proposition, indeed! However, human heads are more than the animal heads, in number. Some of the heads are fearful in appearance and some are so portrayed as if they are lying with their chins touching the ground. A number of examples are having tenons and notches for wearing or hanging. Do these represent the heads which were brought by the victors, i.e., head-hunters, as trophies after defeating their enemies? The winner had to perform a series of rites after he had come home to propitiate the wrath of the vanquished enemy and the wearing of such heads in bone representing the real ones was a part of such a ritual, it appears. From the works of Redfield (1960), Cressman (1960), Montagu (1962), Coon (1967), Catherine H Berndt and Ronald M Berndt (1973) and others, it is evident that head hunting and human sacrifice had been prevalent in many parts of the world since the early days of human civilization. Human sacrifice is recorded in Indus Civilization (Mandal : 1987). In Indian context, references also mention human sacrifice to appease the wrath of Goddess and get Her blessings to achieve success. Goddess Kali is seen to wear garlands of human heads. Again, heads of some folk-level deities are worshipped in our society. Do all these represent the fossil-form of the practice of head-hunting or of the magico-religious belief that has been handed down through ages? Again in 1891, Bishop R. H. Codrington first described a supernatural power of the Pacific Melanesians who called it mana.Belief in such a spiritual or totemic principle is met with among the Australian aboriginals and such ideas are also found all over the world and are called by different names. While explaining the supernatural essence of mana, Montagu writes, "... a stone in the rough shape of some animal, tucked under one's belt, will bring success in the hunt, because of its wonderful power, the mana. (1962 : 163-164)". Perhaps it would not be wrong to guess that under the influence of such a belief, our primitive hunter of this region might have had taken with him a bone depicting an animal with a hope to get success in the hunt. Anthropologists may now analyse and suggest whether these objects representing the human and animal beings are the records of the above practices of the past, in art.

A piece of bone with engravings of two triangular cottages, an animal, a long pole fitted with weapons on one end and surmounted by an animal head, two heads of men and two fabulous beings in flying posture in an attitude to devour them may be taken to record the hazards of a believable jungle-life. The strange beings may represent either some extinct species or imaginary ones of the artist concerned. Presentation of cottages in triangular forms is often met with in art and we may presume that the primitive people of this region led a sort of settled life in a hostile environment of nature. Our artist might have had intended to send some message to somebody living afar. Here we may refer to a 'private letter of an American Indian girl to her lover', as reproduced by A. Montagu (1962:107), as an instance of communication in that hoary past. (Plate-13)

A small beautiful human head to left bears two engraved figures on its forehead. If it is held horizontally with its left border below, a nice female head to right and a strange being with its coiled hinder portion trying to flee away in fear, are engraved. Does the artist want to convey that there is always an inter-play of good and evil or right and wrong in man's mind and he does the good or bad thing whenever anyone wins over ? If it is true, then this example may be said to register man's power of discrimination between good and evil, or right and wrong in a society during the early days of our civilization. (Plate-21)

A few specimens depict two motifs on two sides – one human and one animal. On a specimen a human face is so realistically engraved that, a scholar of Physical Anthropology may be able to determine the stock of people whom the artist imitated. The man depicted might have been the killer and the animal, the killed. However, the artist might have had engraved to commemorate the event at the instruction of the killer. (Plate-110a and 110b)

On another specimen we notice the same kind of engravings. But this time, the human head is shown in profile along the border and the forepart of a dog-like animal is engraved so small that it escapes the notice of an observer. On one side lines of dots depict a being that cannot be understood. Probably, it registers some magico religious belief. (Plate-111a and 111b)

Again, from the realistic execution of phallus symbols, beliefs in fertility cult gain ground. Below a circumcised phallus, the profile of a male human face is carved in antler. It is in someway or other related to fertility cult or it represents the concept of Siva in its earliest form. (Plate-56)

A flattish segment of bone in-the-round is covered with a thin layer of clay and on it are depicted two human figures facing each other very closely. On right is a male and on left, a female. The male figure takes in in his mouth the lips of the female. It is a very natural presentation of coitus, which is very often found on the walls of the Hindu temples of historical periods. (Plate-106)

A black fractured piece of bone pointed at one end, bears a strange human-like face frontally. With lightly engraved two large round eyes, the face wears a fearful appearance of a devil. Most probably it was made for a magic purpose. (Plate-71)

In this connection it may be noted in passing that, though not incorporated in the present monograph, I would like to mention some objects of bones, antlers, animal teeth and shells, characterized by holes or notches that may be taken to represent the examples of adornment. Possibly they were worn independently as pendants or in a group so as to make a necklace or waistband. These are neither carved and engraved, nor painted nor do they depict any motif. Again, belief in magic might have worked for making such objects in order to ward off evil influence that harms man and his pets. A tortoise shell is hung around the neck of a milch-cow by the village folk even today so that milk does not get dried. Here, mention is also made of a flat circular disc of bone (19.3 x 5.6) bearing some enigmatic engravings along its border on the dorsal side. It is significant to note that, in all cases the graver's pointed tool was directed towards the inner field which is evidenced from the shallow lines emerging from each of the engraved symbolic signs spread along the border. We do not know if all these seemingly meaningless engraved signs were a kind of decoration or represented some kind of writing, the legends of which are yet to be deciphered. (Plate-117)

Skill of prehistoric artists displayed in the works of art is amazing. These works, we presume, pleased the people for their 'pleasing forms' and they can compete with the modern art, no doubt. In this regard, attention of our readers may be drawn to the photo plates bearing nos.: 1, 3, 4, 5, 10a, 14, 15, 16, 28, 30, 33, 52, 63, 69, 73, 75, 76 and 110a. Again, depictions are found on the ventral side of the split bones and at times they are in a very diminutive form. Obviously, it was done with a purpose to hide them from the notice of general people. Side view combined with front view, distortion of natural forms, and presence of strange beings are also noticeable. Depictions of all above kinds may be seen in plates bearing nos. : 6, 21, 40, 41, 50, 56, 70, 71, 107 and 111a. Now, on the basis of the concerned works of art we may assert that prehistoric artists were no less gifted than their modern colleagues on the one hand and on the other they themselves being identical with the magicians and priests were obliged to produce the kinds of art that reflect the magico-religious belief imbued with aesthetic fervour.

Thousands of years lie between the people making these works of art and the people appreciating and commenting on them. Both the peoples belong to the completely different sets of societies. All the facets of human society of the past have undergone much change and so quite naturally the approach to the understanding of them gives rise to the divergent sets of opinion. It is quite natural that, the way of living of the members of a society based on hunting-gathering or hunting-gathering and agriculture will differ from that of to-day, which is the evolved form of the former. So the works of art we are dealing with were made either for appreciation or to meet the social purpose of magico-religious belief—which was so essential in the life of man in the then society.

Natshal yields several types of tools including harpoons that indicate older traditions. We are having beautiful examples of tools of the Mesolithic. Neolithic celts are also available here. It is most likely that our ancestors of this region had experienced the warmth of a glowing art tradition. Now we are inclined to note that, the same kind of materials is used to make both tools and works of art, a considerable number of artifacts of above kinds is of same size that corresponds to that of the microlithic industry and the excellence in making them both is irrefutable. These facts seem to establish the probability of their being contemporary and the people who made them were the members of an agrarian society and the works of art, we believe, register on them the stamps of faith, belief and aesthetic ideal of the concerned society, which was Mesolithic in character. Until similar kinds of works of art are available from other sites of Indian subcontinent for comparison and dating, we are hesitant to consider our objects of art to date from the Upper Palaeolithic.

From all the considerations noted above, it appears that though the objects are not stratified examples, they may date from somewhere between the Mesolithic and the end of the Neolithic. To conclude, it may be held that, what has been established about cave and home art in alien countries in respect of forms, styles and ideal, etc., may not be clearly noticeable here for paucity of materials and research. In spite of that, considering the importance and place of such materials in the forward march of human culture, we have tried to interpret the bones in our own way in the present monograph.

Table No. 1

FINAL SCORE-SHEET SHOWING DIFFERENT TRAITS OF WORKS OF ART OF BONE AND ANTLER

Medium		Motif on Bone/Antler						Motif						Techniques							Posture		Posture Suggested		Depiction	
		Cleft bone						Human																		
Bone	Antler	Dorsal side	Ventral side	Bet. Dorsal-ventral	Long bone	Flat Segment	Disc	Male	Female	Difficult	Animal	Pattern	Others	Engraving	Carving	Grinding	Pecking	Cut-out	Painting	Use of clay	Frontal view	Side vies	Standing	Lying	Face/Head	Whole body
118	12	68	13	5	28	12	11	21	8	41	56	3	8	73	58	13	9	6	31	8	28	103	9	8	106	21
90.8	9.2	52.3	10	3.8	21.5	9.2	8.4	16.1	6.1	31.5	43	2.3	6.1	56.1	44.6	10	6.9	4.6	23.8	6.1	21.5	79.2	6.9	6.1	81.5	16.1

1. Measurements are in centimeter.
2. Traits of 7 specimens have been counted twice as either side of them bears depiction.
3. 4 specimens bear depiction on dorsal side extending to the ventral.
4. A number of specimens take more than one column in respect of techniques.

Table No. 2

FLUCTUATIONS OF EXAMPLES OF ART IN RESPECT OF LENGTH AND BREADTH

LENGTH												BREADTH								SPECIMEN
0-3	-4	-5	-6	-7	-8	-9	-10	-11	-12	-13	-14	0-1	-2	-3	-4	-5	-6	-7	-11	
9	15	18	23	15	10	15	3	1	1		1	1	43	33	14	8	10	1	1	111
8.1	13.5	16.2	20.7	13.5	9	13.5	2.7	.9	.9		.9	.9	38.7	29.7	12.6	7.2	9	.9	.9	%
	1	4	2		1	1	2	1	2	1	1									16
			2			1														3

1. Measurements are in cm.
2. Decimal is avoided and measurement in cm. counted to the next higher integer.
3. Where the circular bone disc is broken or it is not completely round its length and breadth are taken.
4. In case of long bone or antler or where sides of a split bone are uneven, only its measurement of length is taken, (16 examples).
5. Measurements of diameter of 3 circular bone discs are taken.

BIBLIOGRAPHY

A. L. Kroeber 1963	Anthropology : Culture Patterns & Processes A Harbinger Book, Harcourt, Brace & World, Inc. New York & Burlingame
Ashley Montagu 1962	Man : His First Million Years A. Signet Science Library Book New American Library
Bridget and Raymond Allchin 1968	The Birth of Indian Civilization, Penguin Books
Carleton S. Coon 1967	The History of Man Penguin Books
David Lambert 1987	The Cambridge Guide to Prehistoric Man, Cambridge University Press, Cambridge
D. H. Gordon 1960	The Pre-historic Background of Indian Culture. N. M. Tripathi (Private) Ltd. 164 - Princess Street, Bombay - 2
Erwin O. Christensen 1960	The History of Wastern Art. A Mentor Book, The New American Library of World Literature, INC. 501 Madison Avenue, New York 22, New Yourk

H. D. Sankalia 1974	Prehistory and Protohistory of India and Pakistan, Deccan College, Postgraduate and Research Institute, Pune
Herbert Read 1949	The Meaning of Art Penguin Books In Association with Faber and Faber
J. Jelinek 1975	The Pictorial Encyclopedia of The Evolution of Man The Hamlyn Publishing Group Limited, Astronaut House, Feltham, Middlesex, England
John Waechter 1976	Man before History Elsevier-Phaidon, Littlegate House, St Ebbe's Street, Oxford
Leonhard Adam 1949	Primitive Art, Penguin Books, Harmondsworth, Middlesex
L. S. Cressman 1960	Man in the New World *In* Man Culture and Society Harry L. Shapiro, Ed. A Galaxy Book New York/Oxford University Press
L. S. B. Leakey 1953	Adam's Ancestors Methuen & Co. Ltd., London 36 Essex Street, Strand, W.C.2
P. K. Mandal 1987	Interpretation of Terracottas from Tamralipta Tamralipta Museum and Research Centre P.O. Tamluk, Dist. Medinipur

P. K. Mandal 1993	Art and Artifacts of Bone and Antler in the Lower Ganges Valley Tamralipta Museum and Research Centre P.O. Tamluk, Dist. Medinipur
M. C. Burkitt 1992	The Old stone Age Rupa & Co. Calcutta
M. C. Burkitt 1929	Our Early Ancestors, Cambridge At the University Press *MCMXXIX*
Percy Brown 1947	Indian Painting, Y.M.C.A. Publishing House, 5 Russell Street, Calcutta
P.C. Das Gupta 1964	The Excavations at Pandu Rajar Dhibi, Directorate of Archaeology, West Bengal, India
P. C. Dasgupta 1981	*Pragaitihasik Bangla*, Anima Prakasani, 141 Keshabchandra Sen Street, Calcutta - 700009
Robert Redfield 1960	How Human Society Operates *In* Man Culture and Society Harry L. Shapiro, Ed. A Galaxy Book New York/Oxford University Press
Sir Edward B. Taylor, KT., 1937	Anthropology: An Introduction to the Study of Man and Civilization London: Watts & Co. 5&6 Johnson's Court, Fleet Street, E.C.4

Sir William Cecil Dampier 1948	A History of Science and its Relations with Philosophy and Religion. The Cambridge University Press (Cambridge, and Bentley House. London)
Stuart Piggott 1950	Prehistoric India Penguin Books. Harmondsworth Middlexex
S. B. Deo 1983	Museum of Archaeology Deccan College Post Graduate & Research Institute, Pune
Asok K. Ghosh 1974	Palaeoanthropology in India *In* Indian Archaeology Today, Dharani Sen, Ed. Dept. of Anthropology, Calcutta University, Calcutta
Olaf H. Prufer 1966	Some Reflections of the Extinctions of the Pleistocene Megafauna *In* Studies in Prehistory. D. Sen and A. K. Ghosh. Ed. Firma K. L. Mukhopadhyaya Calcutta
A Committee of Section H For British Association for the Advancement of Science 1929	Notes and Queries on Anthropology London The Royal Anthropological Institute 52, Upper Bedford Place, W.C.I.

PART - II

PLATES WITH DESCRIPTIONS

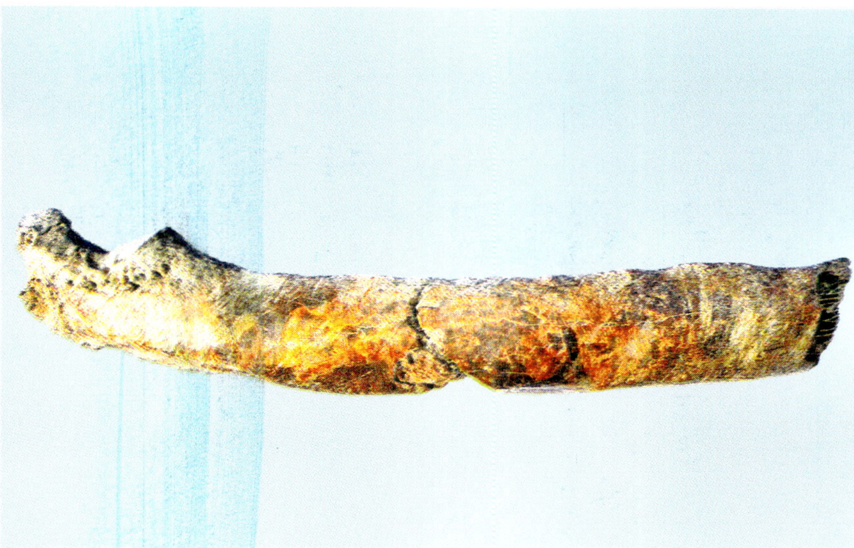

1. Fragmentary portion of a rib (L-14 cm), of a large animal. On it is painted in red and cream a bovine animal standing to left. The head probably rests on the ground and the nose is indicated by the presence of a large circular black dot. The specimen depicted several other motifs which have been obliterated.

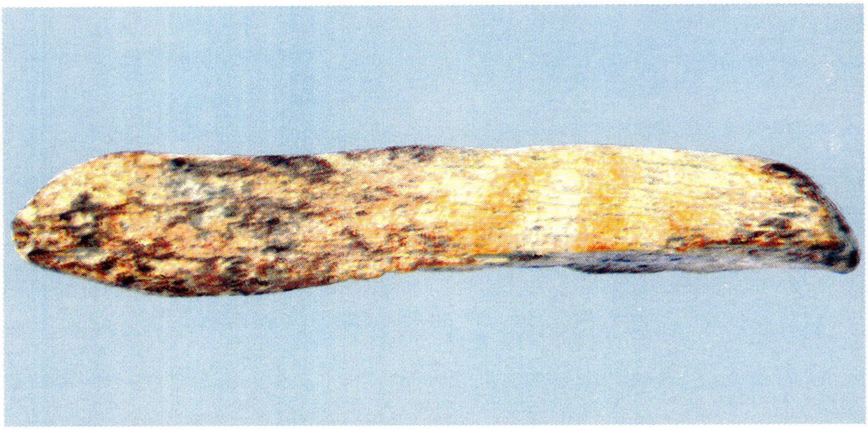

2. The specimen (L-5.5 cm), possibly represents in profile some aquatic being to left. It is painted in red with vertical lines on the dorsal side only. The eye on left is painted in black. Some portion below is broken.

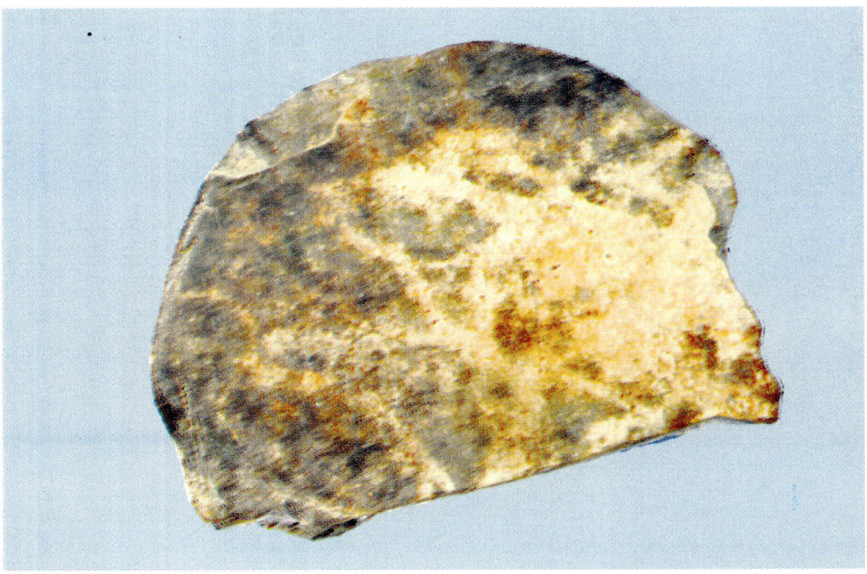

3. The semicircular specimen (5.2 x 4.1 cm), bears painting on its dorsal side. Against the red background a running horned bovine animal to left is painted in creamish white.

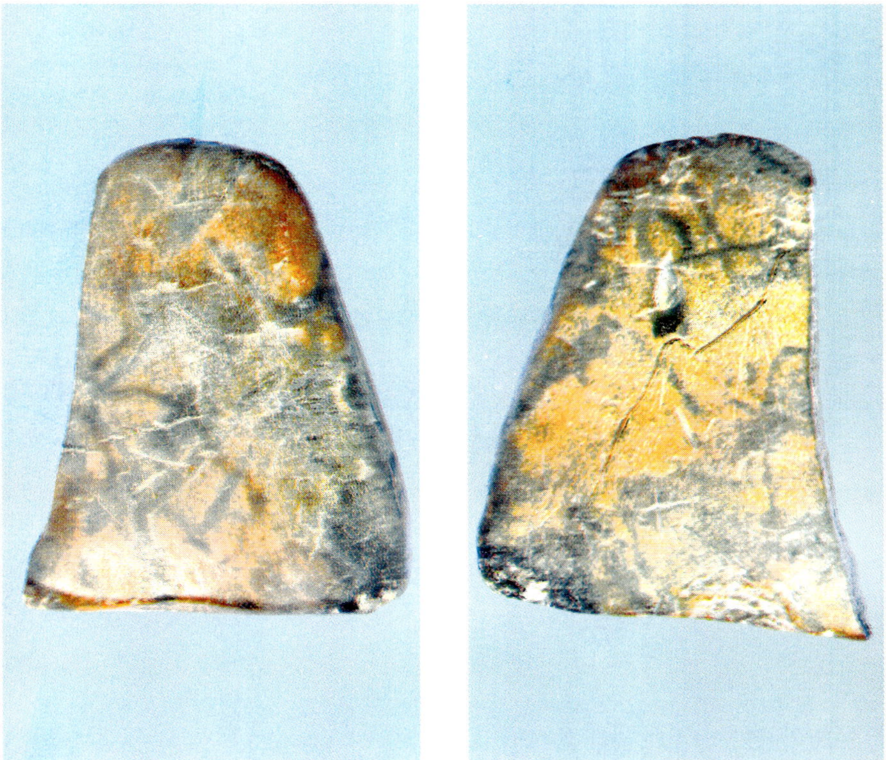

4. The specimen (5.8 x 4.6 cm), in the shape of a Neolithic celt bears both painting and engravings on either side. While on one side is shown a bovine animal turning its head back as if licking its hinder part, on the other side is shown another beast presented in the same posture. Colour used are black and red. Again shallow engraved lines are noticeable but they do not seem to follow those of painted motifs. The interesting point to note is the shape of the specimen and on the basis of its similarity with a Neolithic celt one may like to attribute to it a Neolithic or Chalcolithic date.

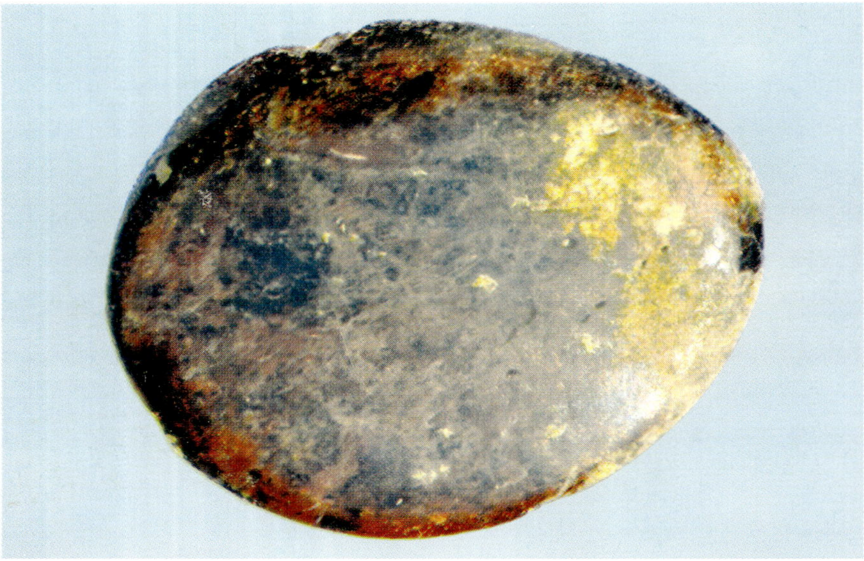

5. The thick disc of bone (6.5 x 5.5 cm), almost circular in outline bears painting on the dorsal side only and on the ventral side in the middle occurs what appears to be the head of some human being in profile to right in low relief. However, on the dorsal side against the common pale red background, an animal is painted in profile to left. The outline and hair of the concerned animal are painted in black and it appears to represent a lion.

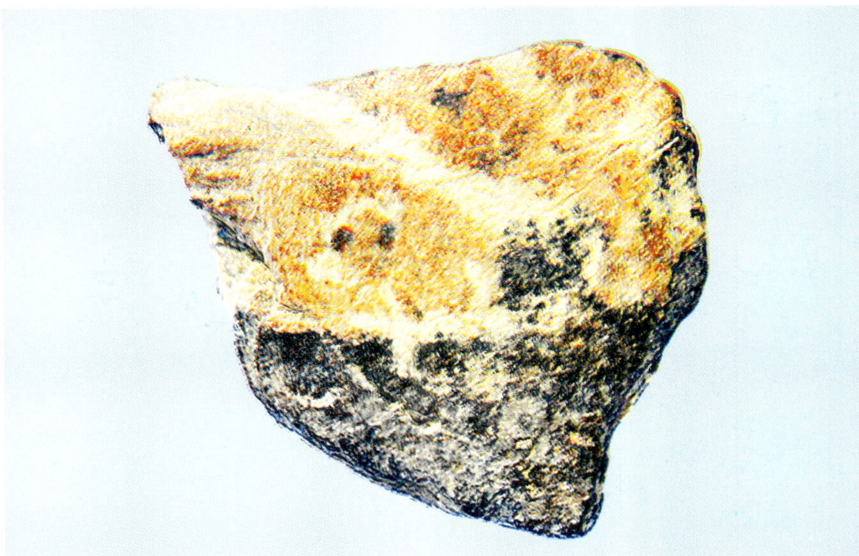

6. Only the forepart of an animal head in profile to right is painted on this small specimen (2.6 x 2.1 cm). The animal probably represents a dog. Red, black and white colour are used.

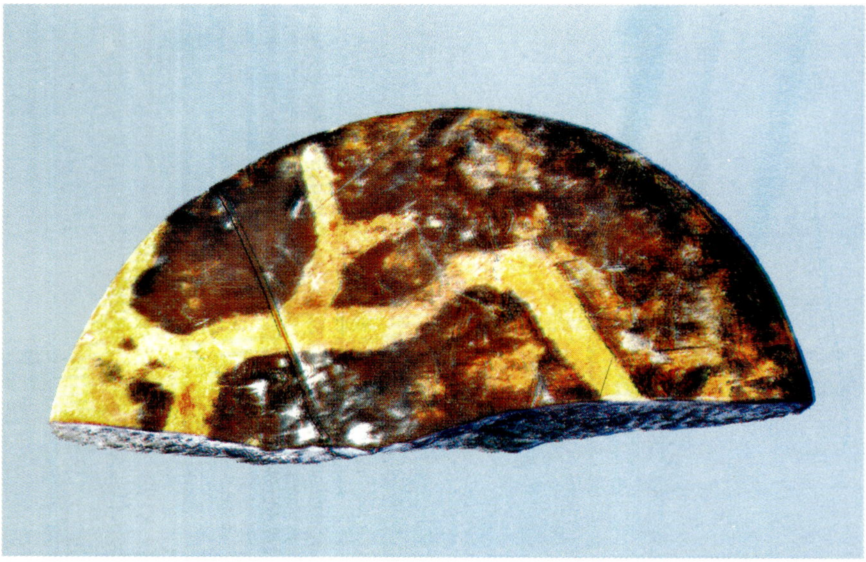

7. The specimen (8.5 x 4 cm), in two pieces represents only one half of a circular disc of bone, bearing paintings on the dorsal side. The motif in cream colour is painted against the background in deep red. Probably the motif depicts one half of a branched antler and the other half is missing due to mutilation of the disc.

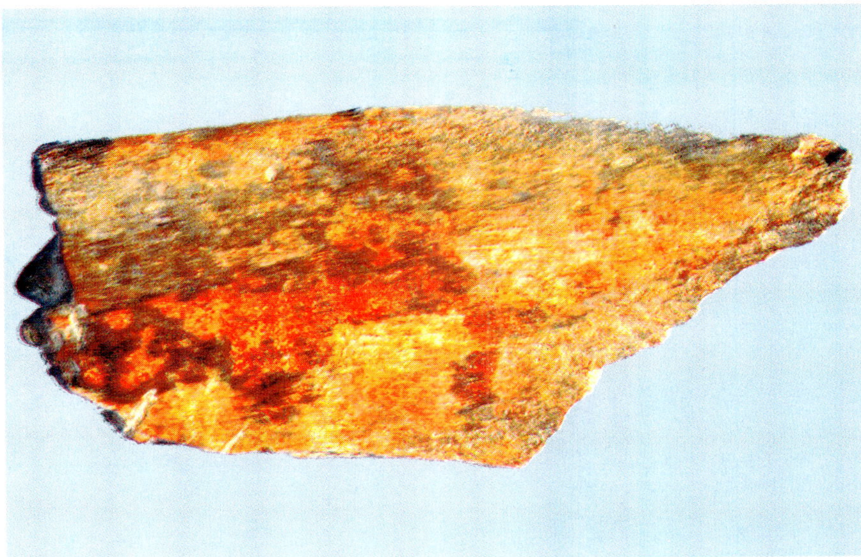

8. The specimen (7 x 3 cm) depicts three animals in red and black. The animal in front has its tail coiled on right and the head placed full-face on left. Presence of two other animals is suggested by their heads on left, while their bodies, as it appears, are hidden behind the former one. One of the latter two heads is painted in profile in likeness of a human head on extreme left and the other of a fox-like animal painted full-face in the middle. Further other than the coiled tail mentioned earlier another tail like member on right confirms the suggestion of the presence of more than one animal in the depiction. Probably the figure on extreme left may be a human being in disguise imitating the postures of two other animals as a part of some kind of magico-religious rite.

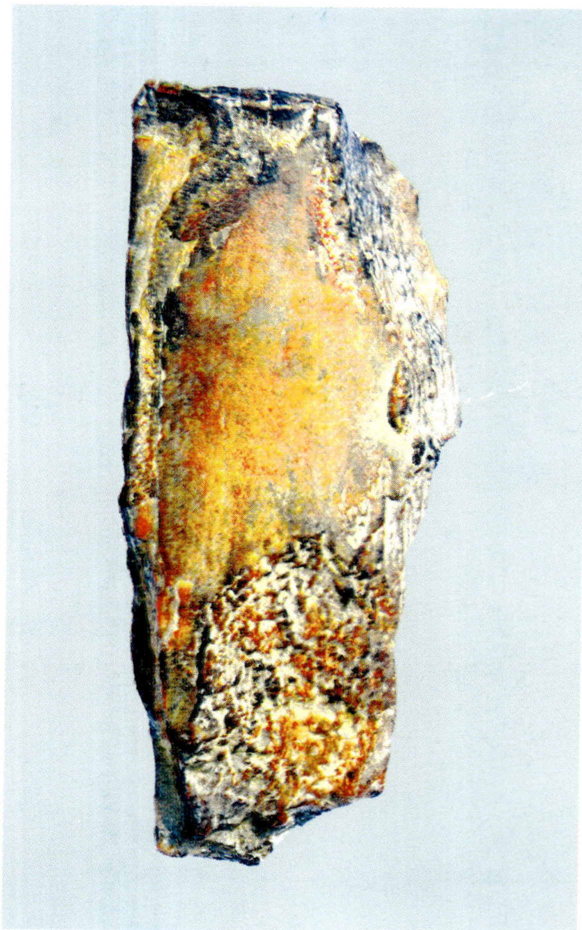

9. The flat segment (7.4 x 3 cm), bears on its dorsal side the depiction of an animal in red with its face turned to left a little. What is important here to note is that the figure is painted showing no legs, ears, eyes, mouth and nose etc..

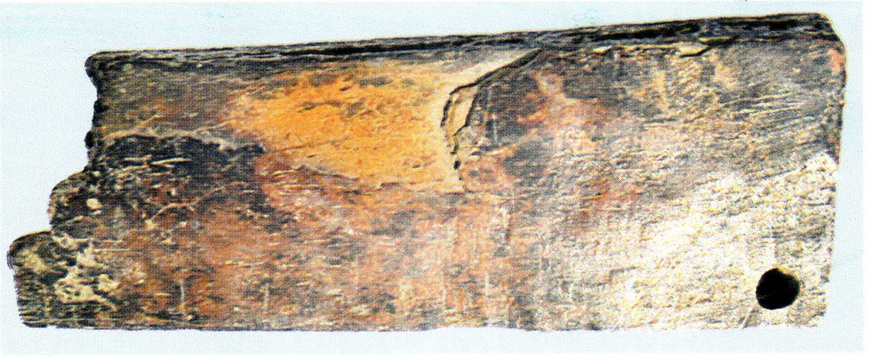

10. On this smooth and thick rectangular piece of bone (8.2 x 3.2 cm), a beast is seen reclining with its head on right. The beast in low relief turns its head back and it is painted in red and black. A large hole on right below is for hanging.

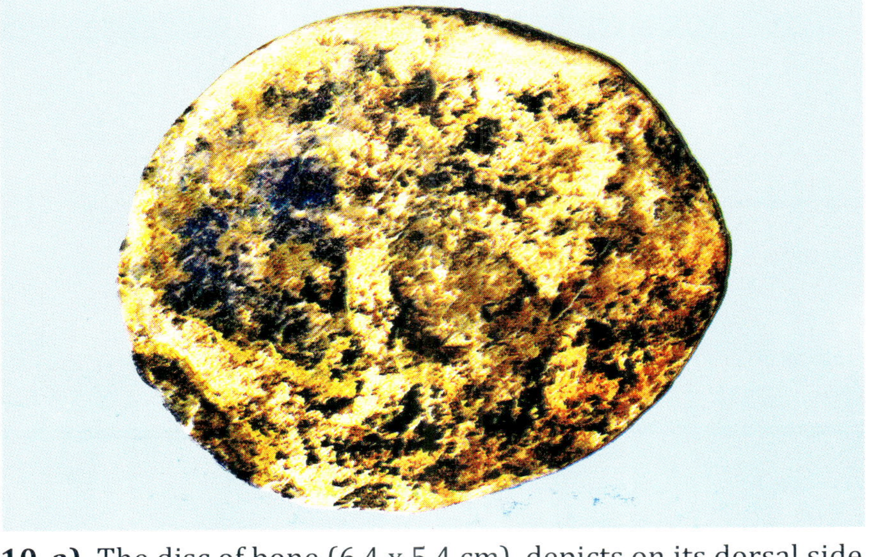

10 a). The disc of bone (6.4 x 5.4 cm), depicts on its dorsal side two animal heads in black against a cream background. The heads apparently resemble those of bears. While one of them is painted frontally, the other is seen in side-view. Another animal in cream is painted to right. All the animals are so neatly placed that the viewer has little difficulty in identifying them individually. The ventral side is painted in black totally.

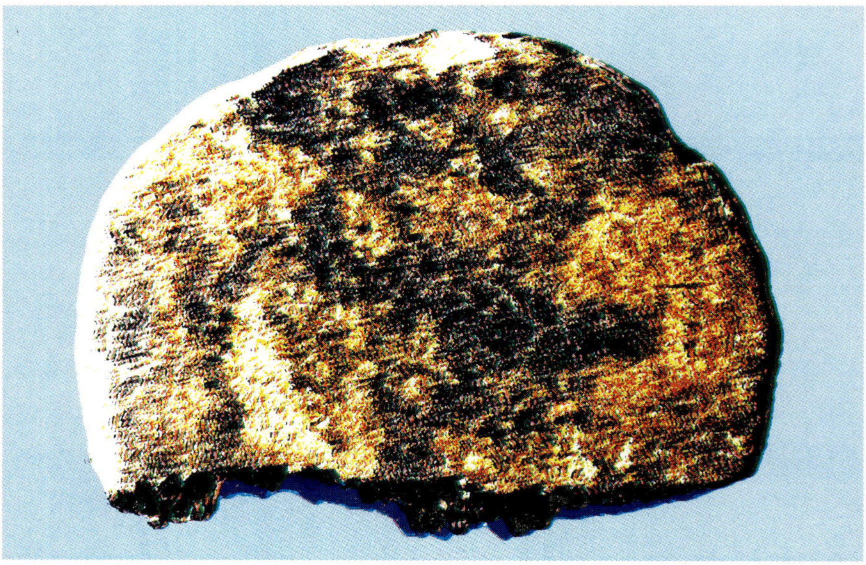

11. On this fragmentary portion of a disc of bone (5.3 x 3.7 cm), two animals are painted in black. While the one above is depicted as standing to left, the other with its long tail is shown to right below. Both of them are, as if , in moving attitude

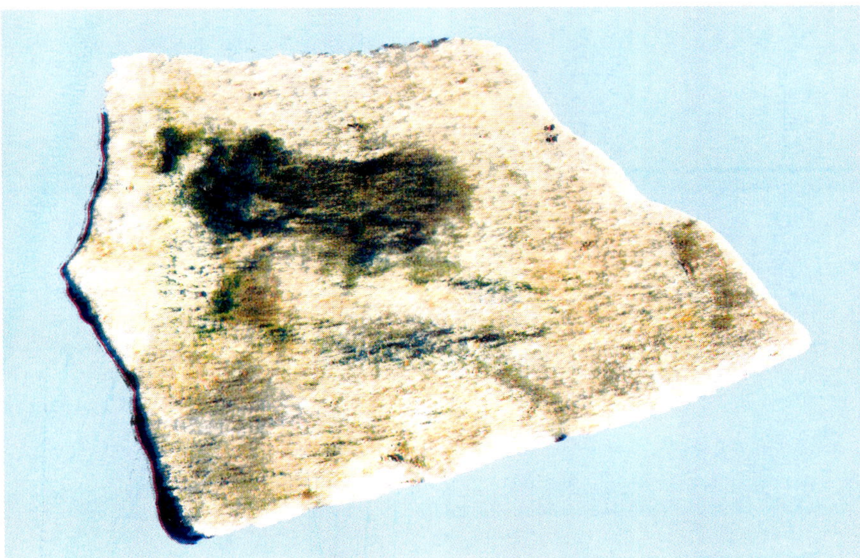

12. It is a small and thin piece of sand stone (7.7 x 6.1 cm). It hails from the same site of Natshal. On it an animal in profile to left is painted in black. Superimposition is noticeable. Paintings below are obliterated. The animal seems to represent a bull. From overall impression it appears to appertain to the Neolithic.

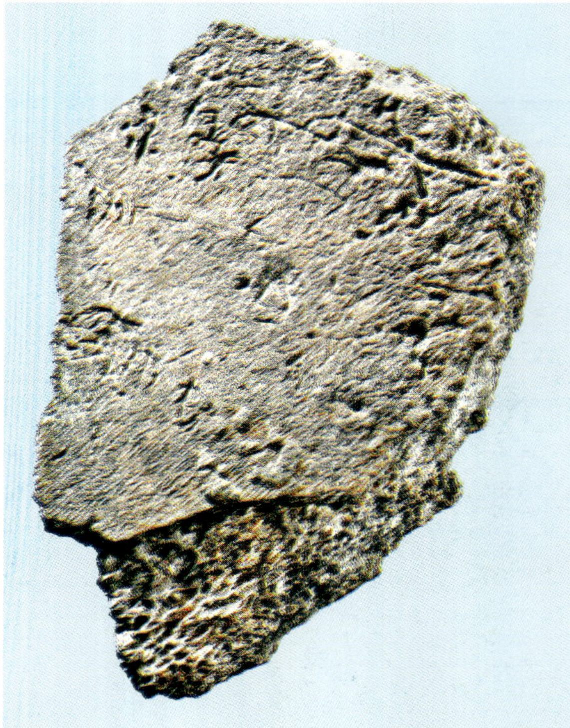

13. It is almost a triangular thick piece of bone (8.2 x 5.5 cm), depicting strange animals, human heads, and triangular cottages, engraved. Two human beings represented by their heads in profile to right are attacked from right by two strange beings. While one of the heads above is being devoured by one of the beings, the other below is face to face with a larger being. The beings are as if in flying posture. Below them is engraved a pole fastened with two chisel-like weapons on which rests an animal head. Again below the pole are seen two triangular engravings, probably signifying cottages and on left the full figure of an animal in profile to left. Certainly the specimen conveys some appalling theme hinted at by the presence of frightened humans, two strange beings, a weapon with an animal head and a beast.

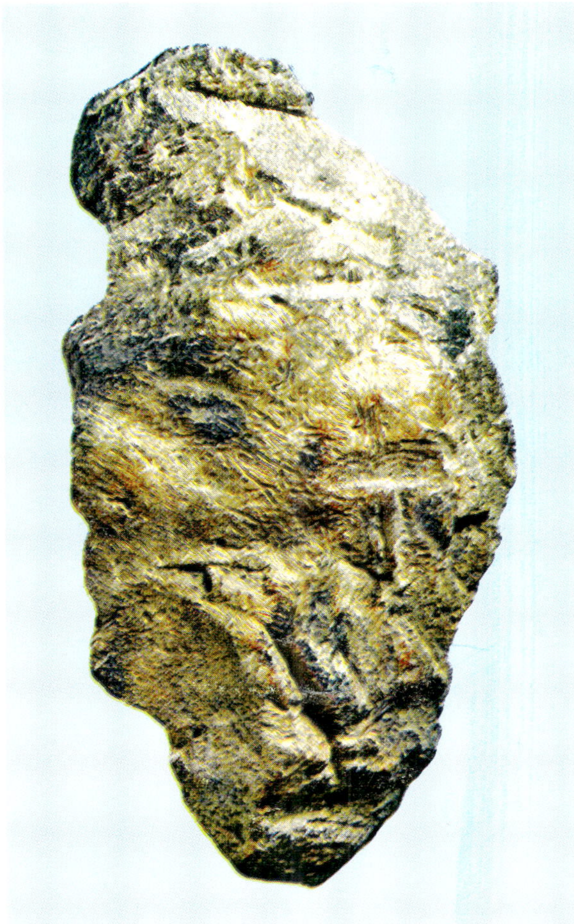

14. The sculpture (8 x 4.2 cm), depicts almost frontally a face with wide open mouth. This open-eyed grotesque face shows its nose schematically represented. The forehead is enough broad and receding. Probably the notch above is meant for hanging. The deeply cut-marks were effected by heavy-duty tools.

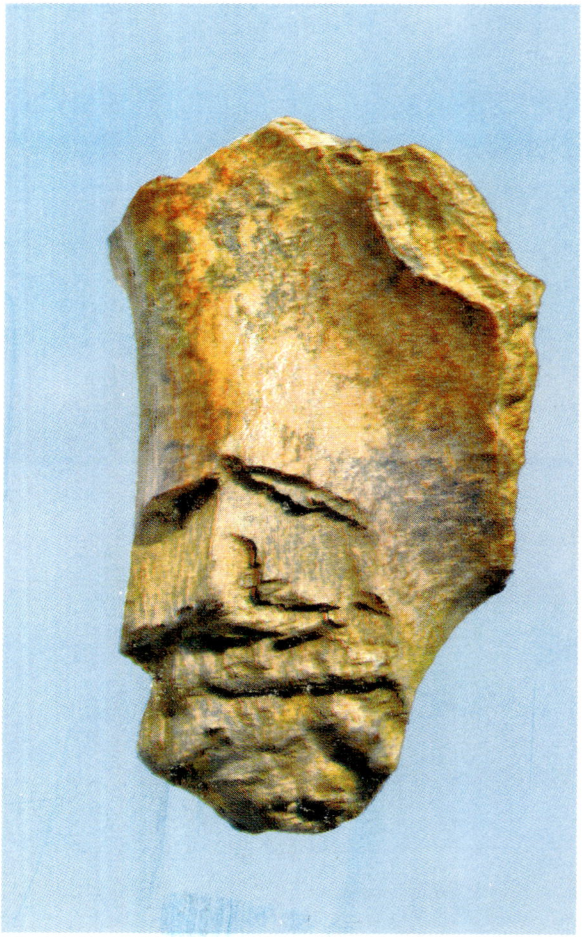

15. It is a three-dimensional presentation of a human head on bone (5.8 x 3 cm). Flakes are removed from either side of the nose that mark the parts of cheek. Upper and lower lips with a horizontal engraving signifying mouth are well marked. Probably the man is having beard.

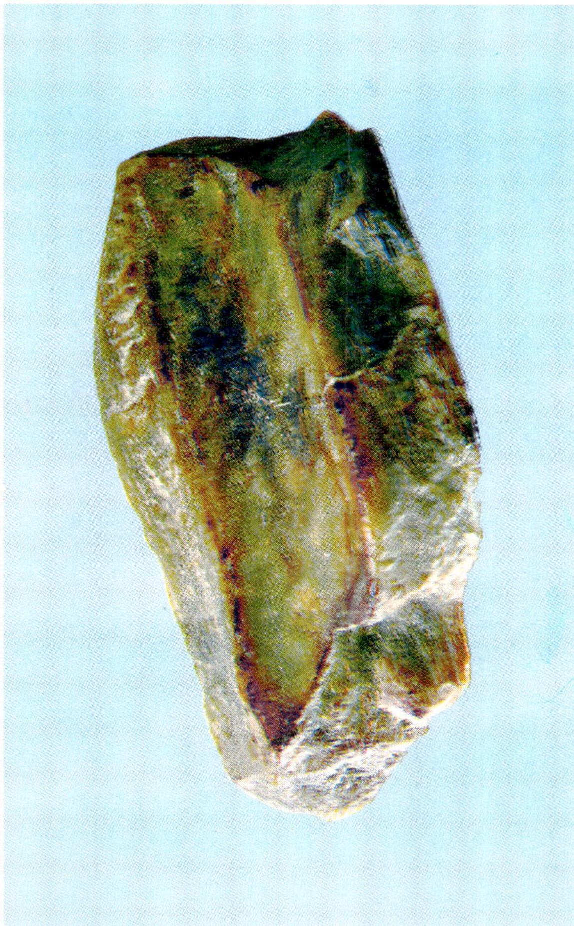

16. It is a small cleft segment of bone (4 x 2.3 cm), mineralized. Small nose, cheek and open mouth, almost triangular, of a human face are nicely carved on the ventral side covering the section between the dorsal and ventral side on right. Physical traits are interesting.

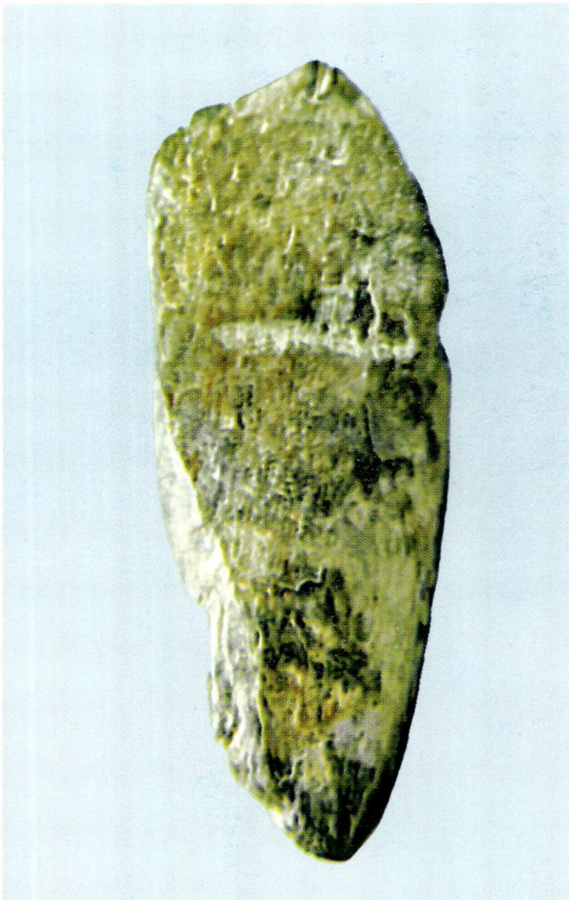

17. A black and flat segment of bone (5 x 1.9 cm) representing a human head. Along its left border, the face to left in profile is carved including the forehead, nose and lips. An engraved horizontal line seems to mark the end of its forehead above and a notch to its right probably facilitated binding it to a rope for wearing or hanging.

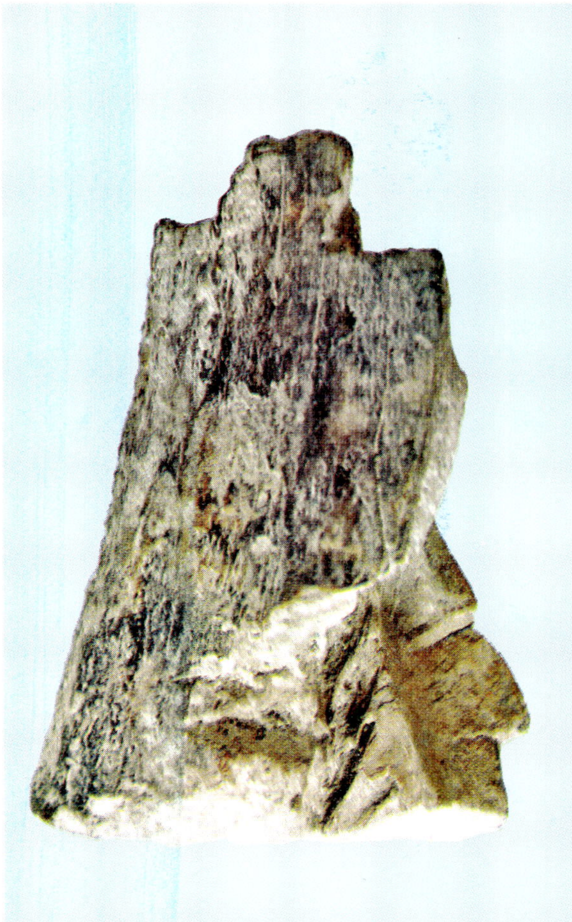

18. On this small piece of bone (4 x 2.5 cm), forehead, ridge of eye-brow, prominent nose and chin of a human face are nicely carved along the right border. Notch above is probably for hanging.

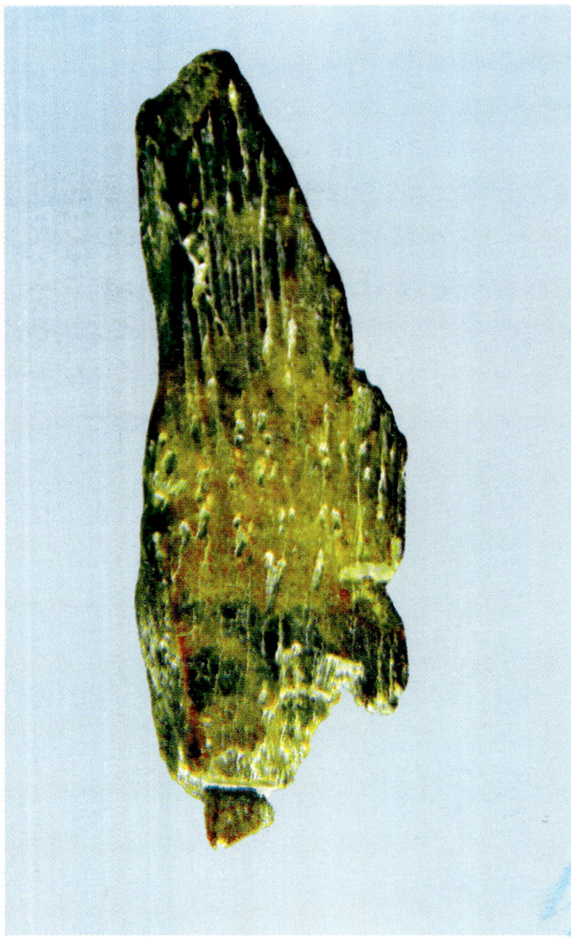

19. The figure (3.5 x 1.2 cm), portrays human face to right. The forehead, broad and prominent nose and chin are executed along the right border. The portion beyond the head above gradually tapers to a point.

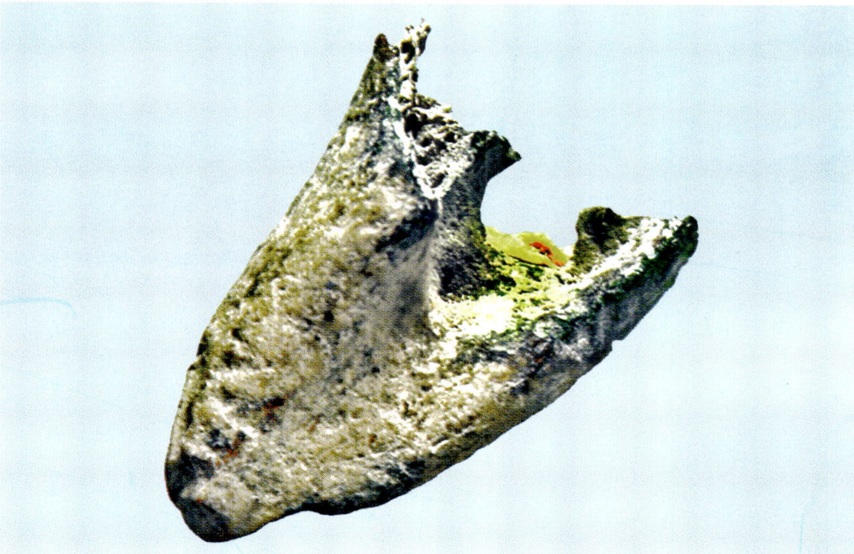

20. It is a hollow piece of bone (2.6 x 1.7 cm), depicting a human face in profile to left. Flesh on cheek is well delineated. Eyes and open mouth are well carved. Notch above is probably for hanging.

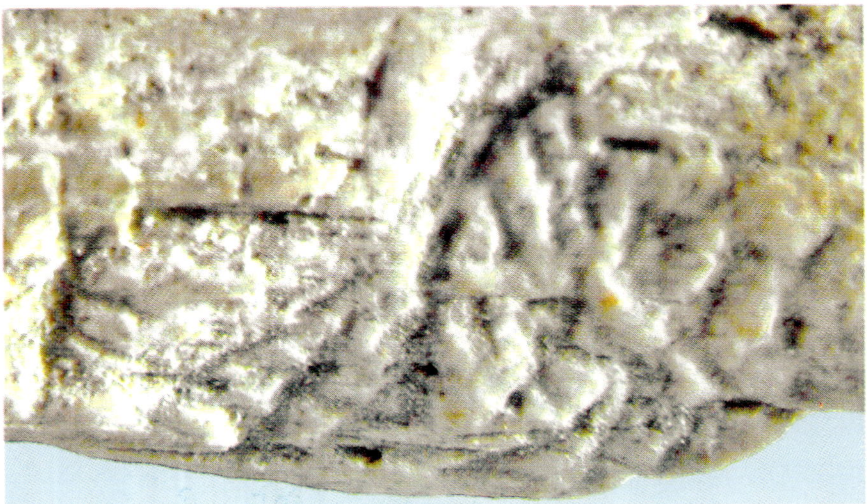

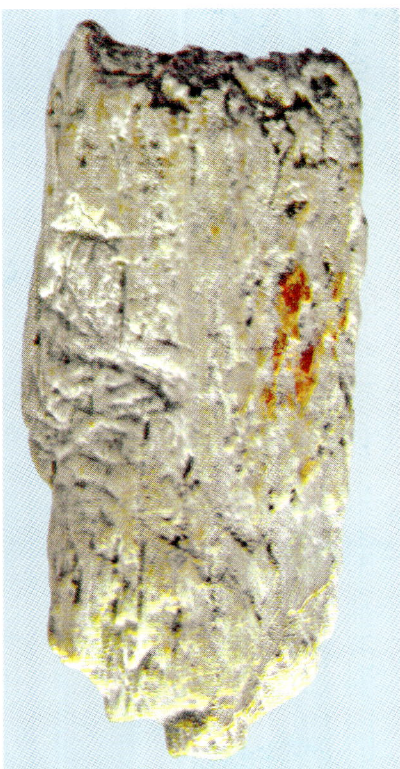

21. The specimen (2.7 x 1.1 cm), depicts a human head in Profile to left. Along the border on left, long nose and mouth are beautifully carved. The profile is shown on the dorsal side of the cleft bone. On the forehead above nose, two motifs are engraved. If the specimen is held horizontally with its left border below, the profile of a human face to right is noticeable. On its right is engraved a strange being frontally with its twisted and coiled hinder portion.

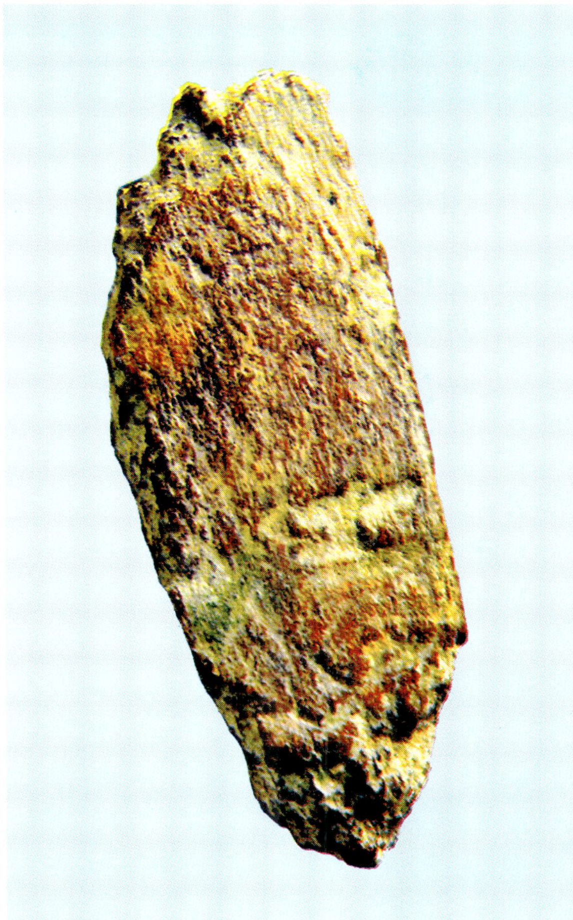

22. This small segment of bone (2.2 x .8 cm), depicts a human head in profile to right. Eye, nose and mouth with thick lips are well engraved.

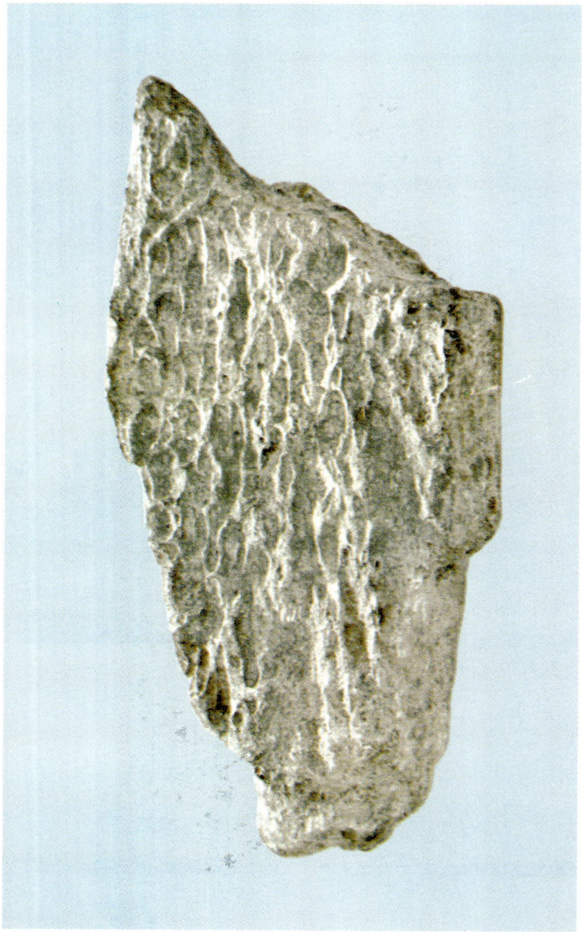

23. On this small fractured segment of bone (3.5 x 1.6 cm), lower lip of a human being is nicely executed on its ventral side but all other features of face are totally absent.

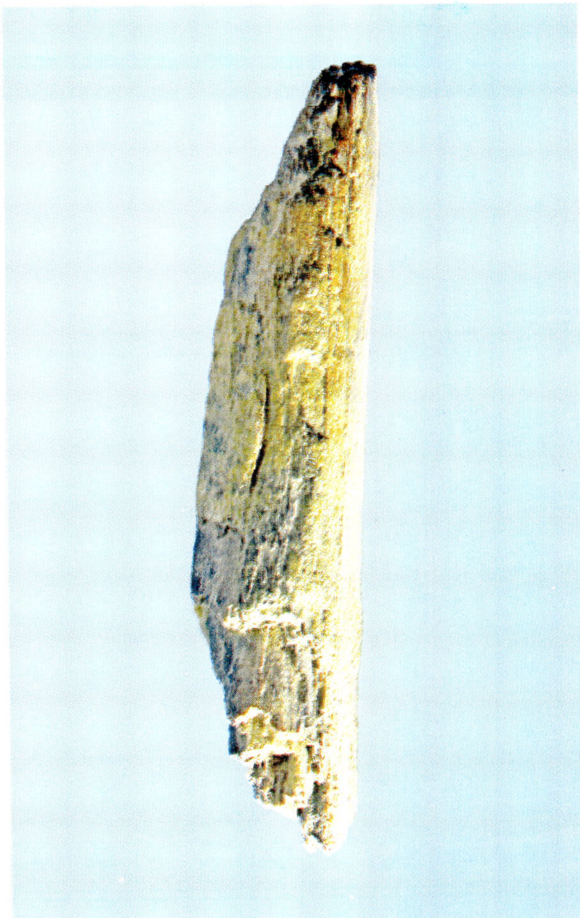

24. The specimen (5.2 x 1.3 cm), illustrates a human head. While the right half of the dorsal side remains untouched, its left half depicts the face to left in profile. Long nose, wide open mouth and chin are carved. A bit of bone has been scooped out to make the cheek and eye socket. The forehead gradually recedes backward.

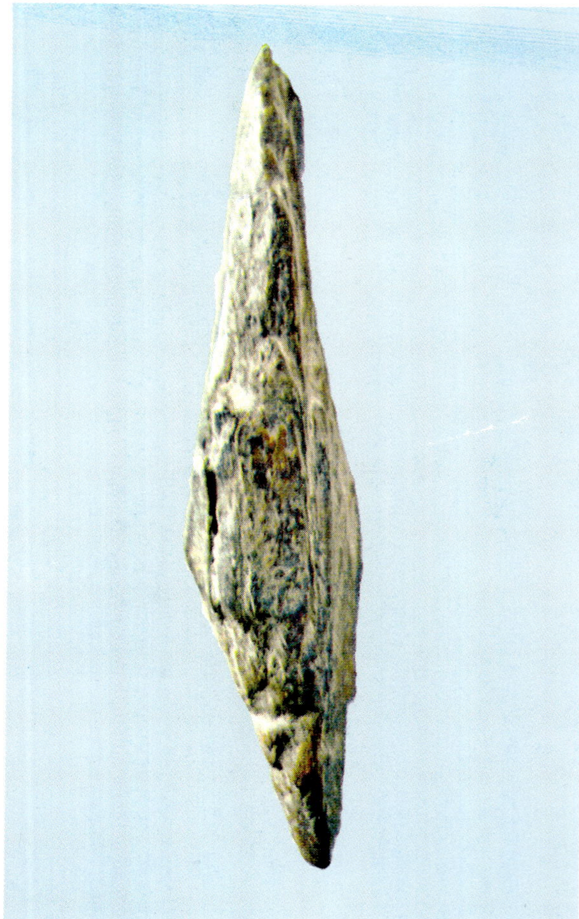

25. In this small piece of bone (L-4.7 cm), mouth and chin are marked by engraving. The tapering portion above is meant for hanging.

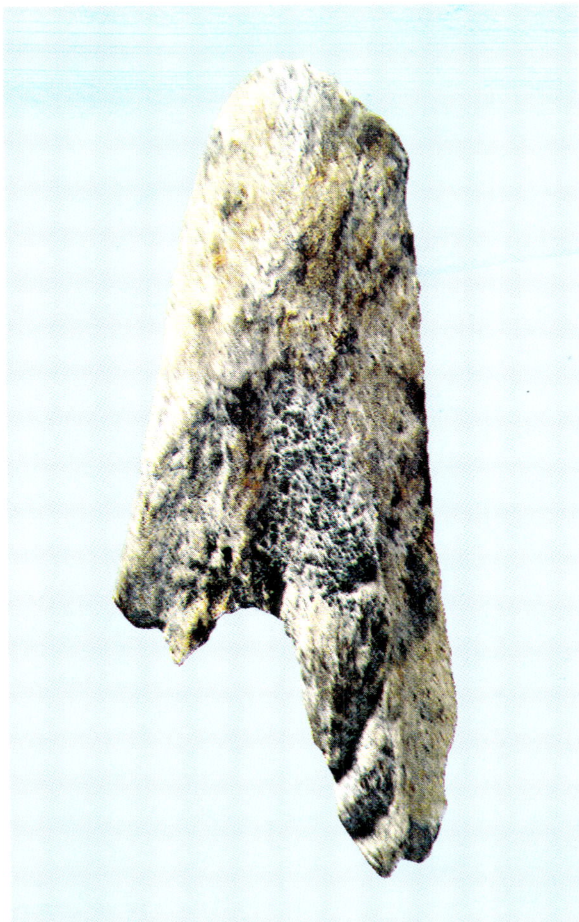

26. On the right branch of a cleft bone (4.7 x 1.8 cm), eye, nose and thick lips of a human being are carved in profile to left. It probably represents a female face.

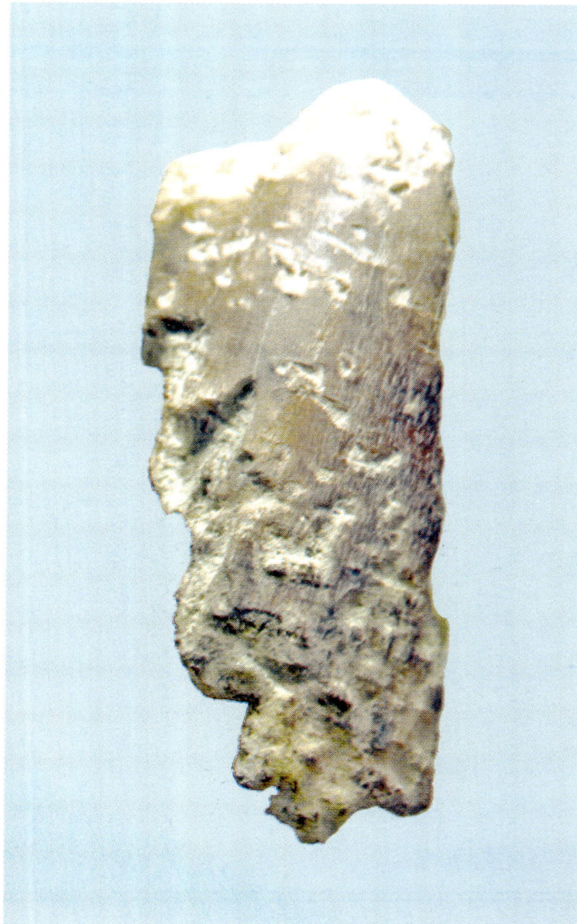

27. Face of a man to left on a small piece of bone (4.4 x 1.4 cm), is engraved. Marks of pecking all over the face are noticeable. We do not know it for certain whether these marks are for ornamentation or they signify the prevalence of pox at the time of portrayal of the concerned motif or they represent some form of magic art.

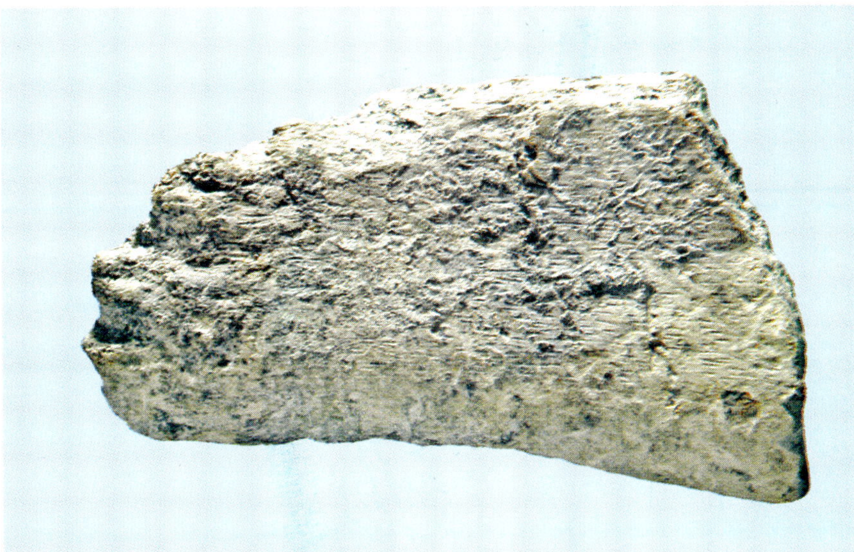

28. The small segment of bone (4.1 x 2.6 cm), represents the side-view of a female face. Along the left border are executed the round eyes, nose, upper and lower lips and chin from above respectively. A short vertical cut-mark indicates the end of the forehead. The head is, as if, lying with its chin resting on the ground.

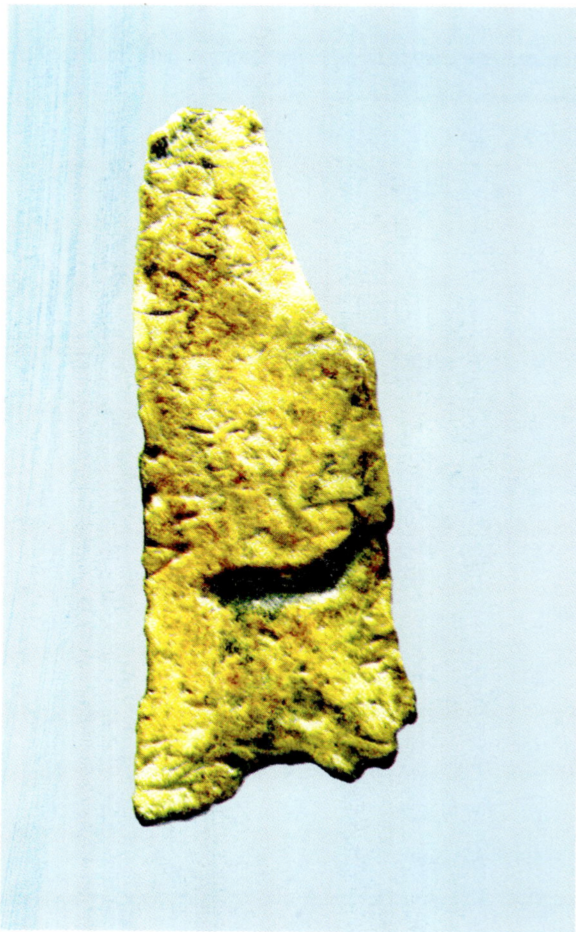

29. Bust of a human being in profile to right is engraved along the right border of the thin piece of cleft bone (7.3 x 3.1 cm). Eye, nose, lips and chin are well defined and engraved. The man is, as if, in lying posture. Outline of the portion separated by engraving gives the impression of an animal head above.

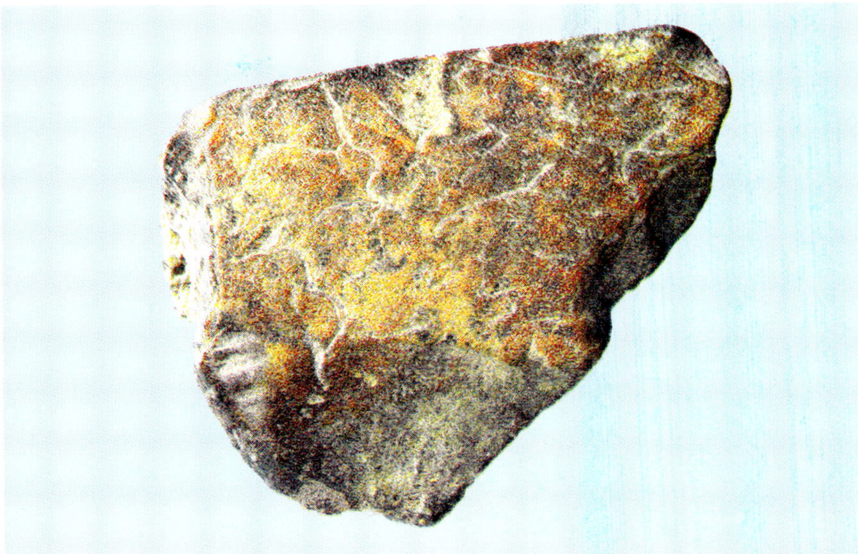

30. Eyes, nose and mouth of a man are shown on the left border of the small piece of bone (2.5 x 2.1 cm). It is an excellent work of art.

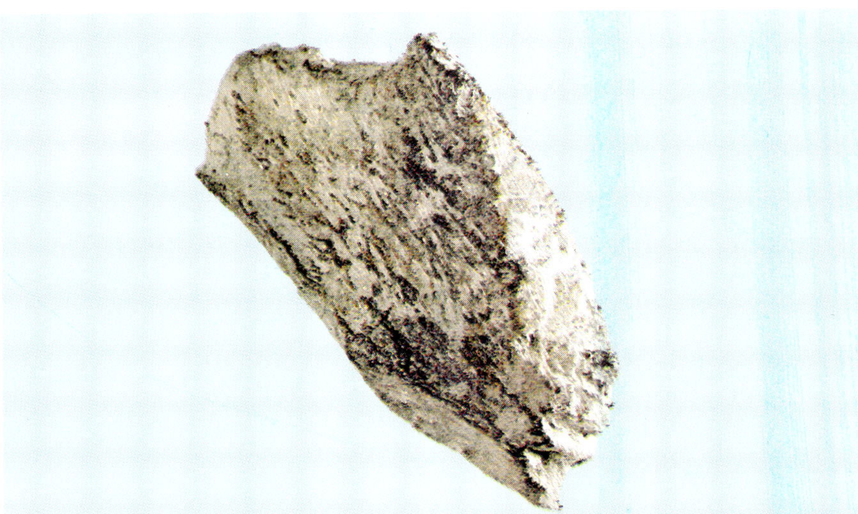

31. The specimen (3.2 x 1.9 cm), depicts the face to right along the carved border on right.

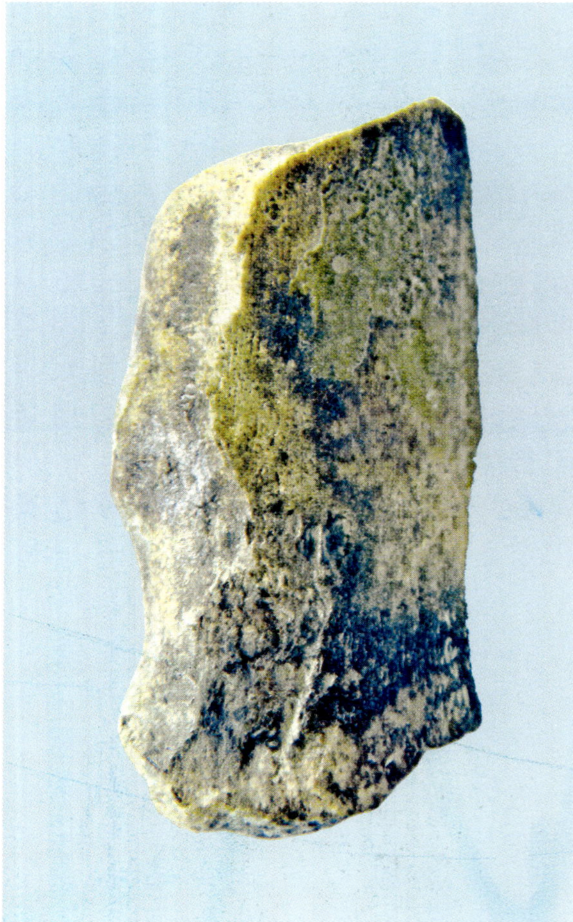

32. The face is in profile to left. Snub nose without its bridge and the mouth are carved. The specimen (3.6 x 2 cm), is a good piece of carving.

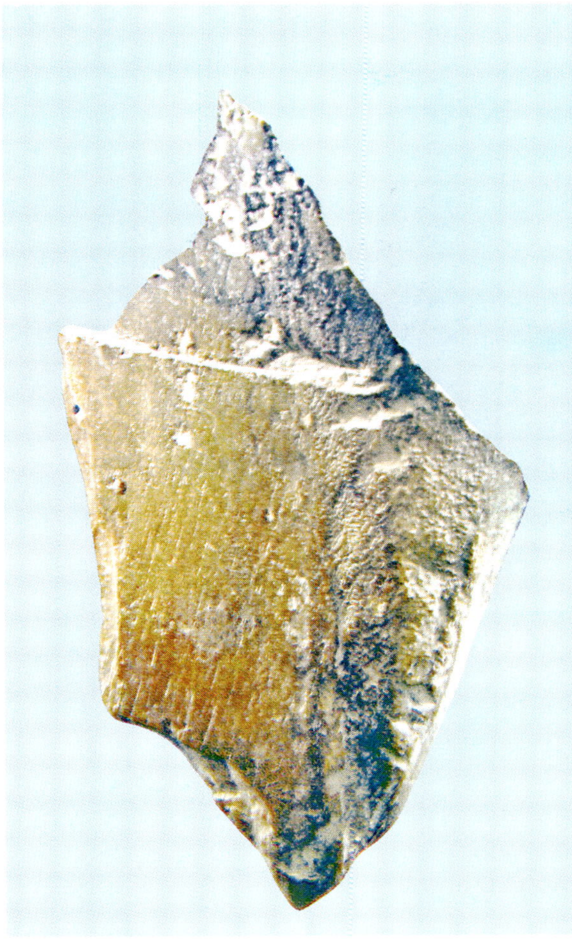

33. Fractured and broken piece of bone (5 x 3 cm). Dorsal side is oval. Right side of a human face is beautifully carved in bas-relief to right. It is characterized by broad forehead, long nose and thick lower lip.

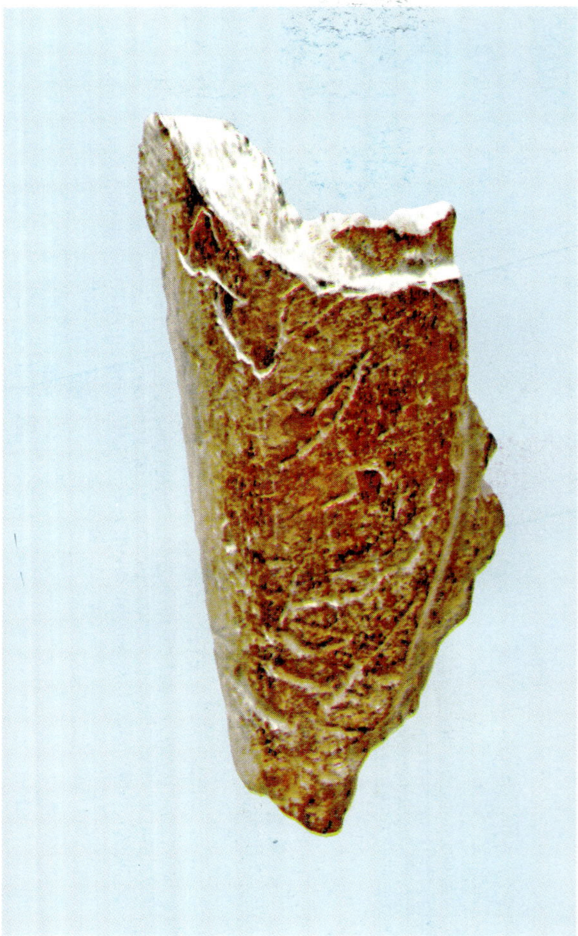

34. Fractured and broken piece of bone (5 x 2 cm). Dorsal side is oval. Outline of a human face is nicely engraved. Chin and mouth are well marked.

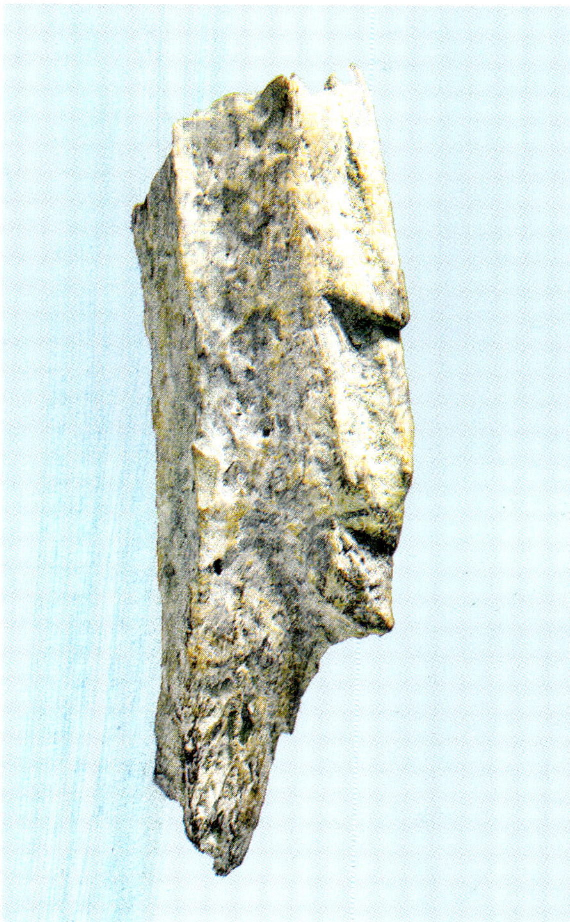

35. A human face is depicted on the ventral side of a cleft and fractured piece of bone (6.3 x 2.2 cm). The forehead, long nose and tapering chin are brought out by taking off flakes from the ventral side on the right border.

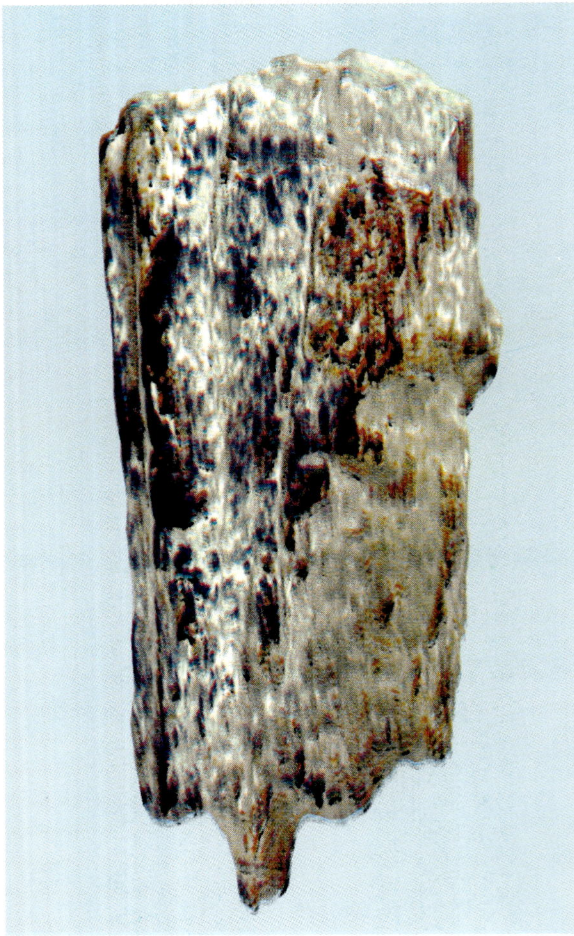

36. The forehead, unusually long nose and the mouth with tapering lower lip are seen on the right border. Its cheek is done by scraping. The specimen (3.6 x 1.5 cm), is black.

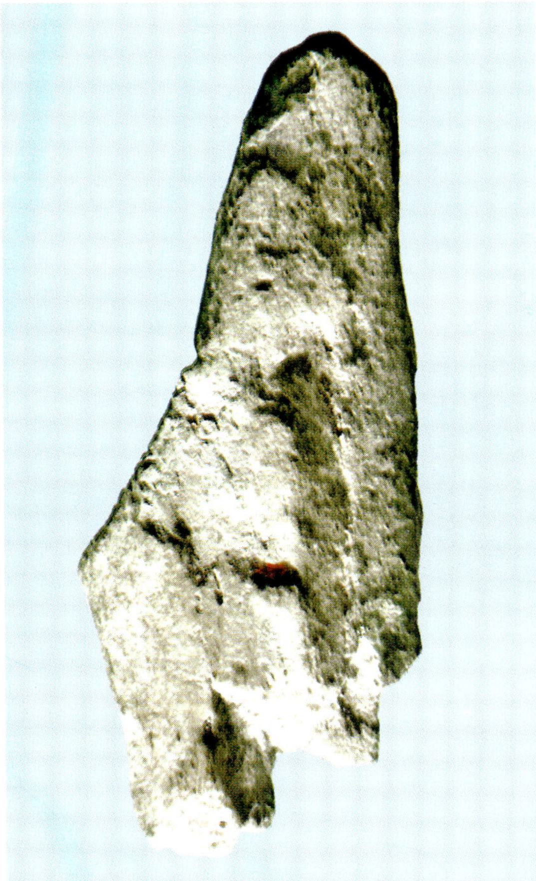

37. The specimen (4.5 x 1.8 cm), represents the side view of a human face. Three vertical strips, parallel to each other, are noticeable on the dorsal side of the bone. The narrower strip on right sinks down below the surface due to carving. This part covers the forehead and nose without any distinctive mark separating them. The strip in the middle represents the face from nose to ear, with a short deep horizontal engraving for the right eye. Again the third one on extreme left certainly stands for the lower jaw and the chin. The mouth below is shown by the removal of a triangular segment from the lower end of the middle strip – forming an angular gap between the second and the third strips. However, the overall appearance of the face is appalling and such type of heads may be compared to a class of grotesque heads of contemporary folk gods. It appears, such objects were fashioned for wearing, as is suggested by the remaining portion of bone above the forehead. Possibly they were used in order to ward off evil influence.

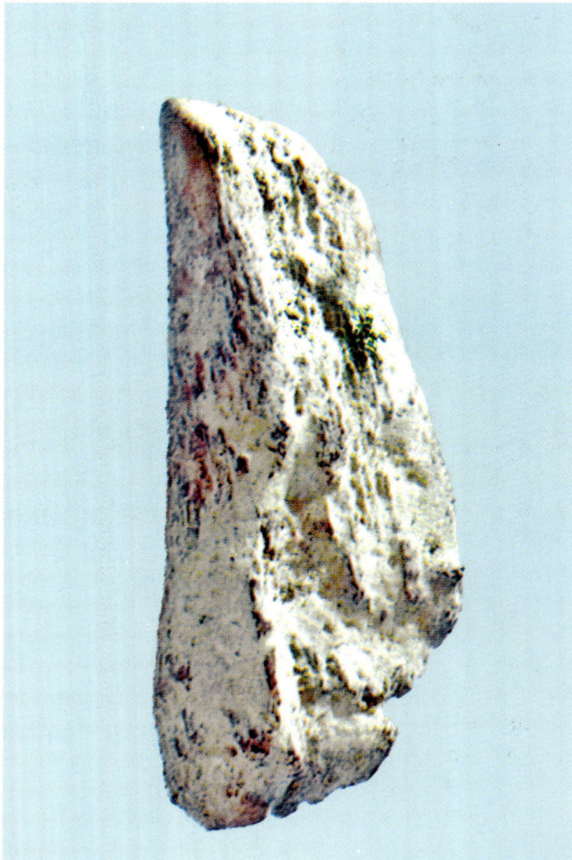

38. The specimen (3.5 x 1.4 cm), depicts on its ventral side the profile of a human head. Characteristic physical traits as observed are a broad nose and heavy fleshy lips. The head above is tapering and elongated, probably for binding with a rope for hanging.

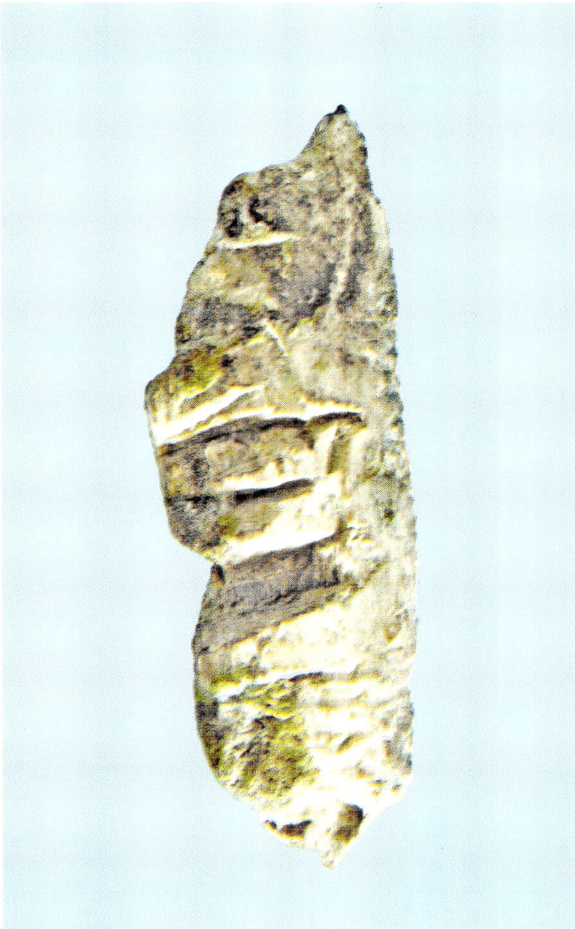

39. Deeply engraved horizontal lines mark the forehead, lips and mouth. The nose is well marked. The face is in profile to left. It is on the hollow cylindrical segment of bone (L-4 cm).

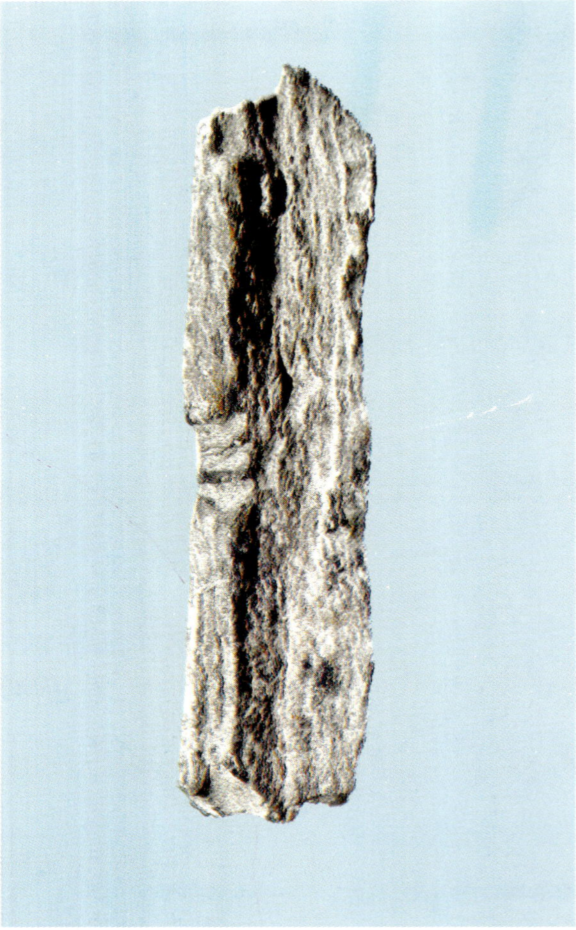

40. On the ventral side of a cleft and fractured piece of bone (7 x 1.6 cm), the nose, lips and mouth of a human being are carved along the left thick border. Eye is also indicated.

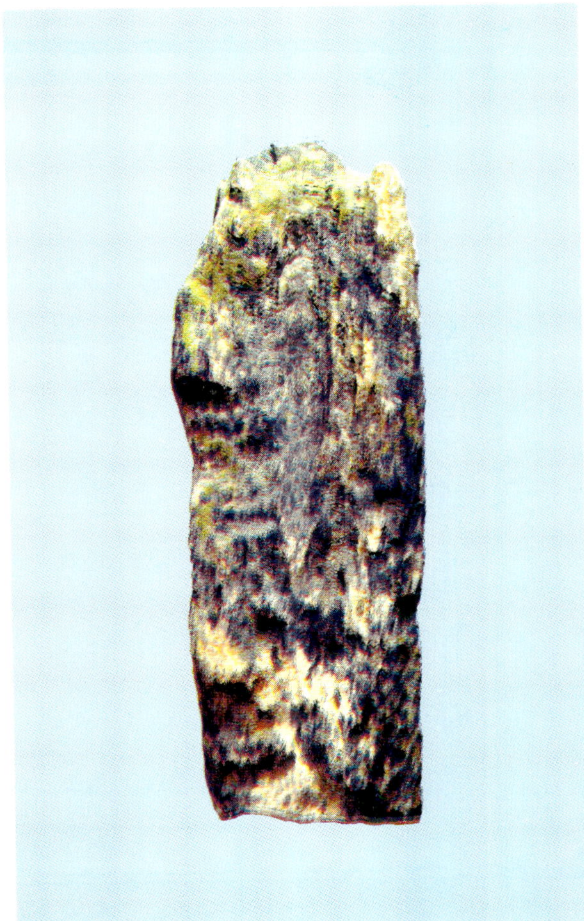

41. Two human faces are depicted on the ventral side of the cleft segment of bone (5 x 1.7 cm). One above is in three-fourths frontal view to right. Open mouth, nose and eyes are seen. The other is in profile to right along the left border below.

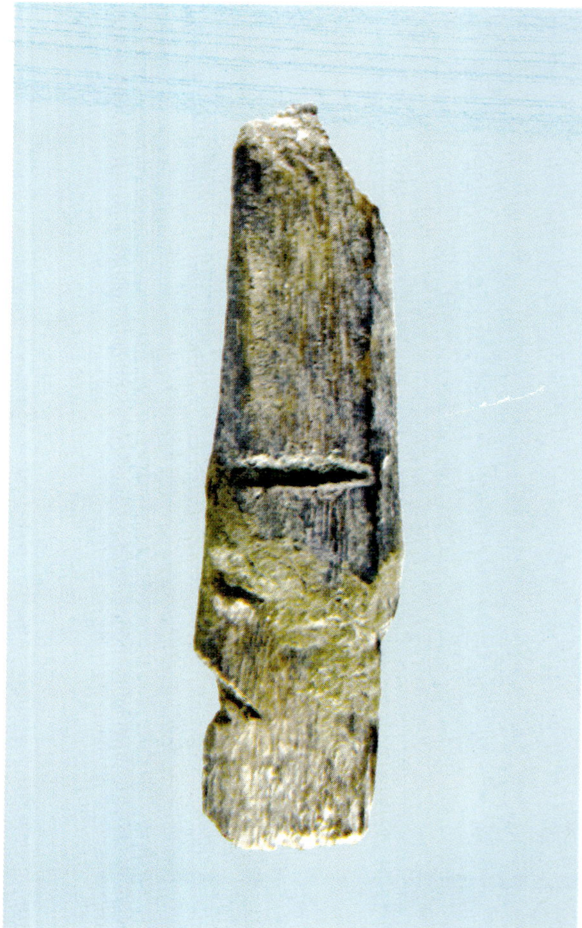

42. A long segment of bone (4.3 x 1.1 cm), depicting a human head in formal profile to left. A deeply cut horizontal line separates the head from the unused portion of bone above. The eye and the mouth are well marked. Across the temple passes a fillet-like member of gritty clay that seems to be bound in a knot behind the head.

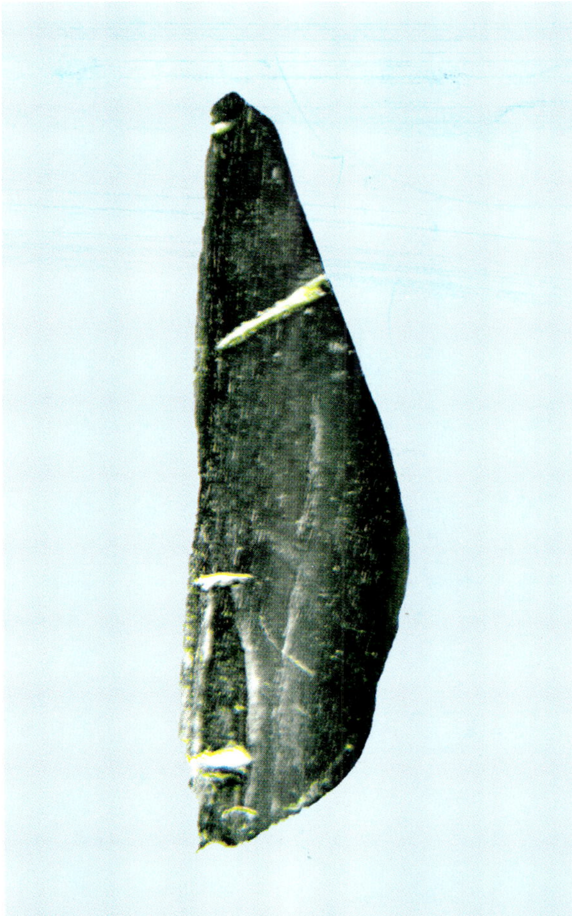

43. A triangular segment of bone (4.3 x 1.3 cm), black in colour, representing probably a human face in three-fourths frontal view. While a little oblique engraved line marks the end of the head above, two short incised lines mark the end of the forehead and the nose below respectively. The characteristic features of the specimen are: (i) the nose is shown in low relief, and (ii) the eyes and the mouth are absent.
However, absence of eyes and mouth etc., does not seem to be any hindrance in taking it for a face.

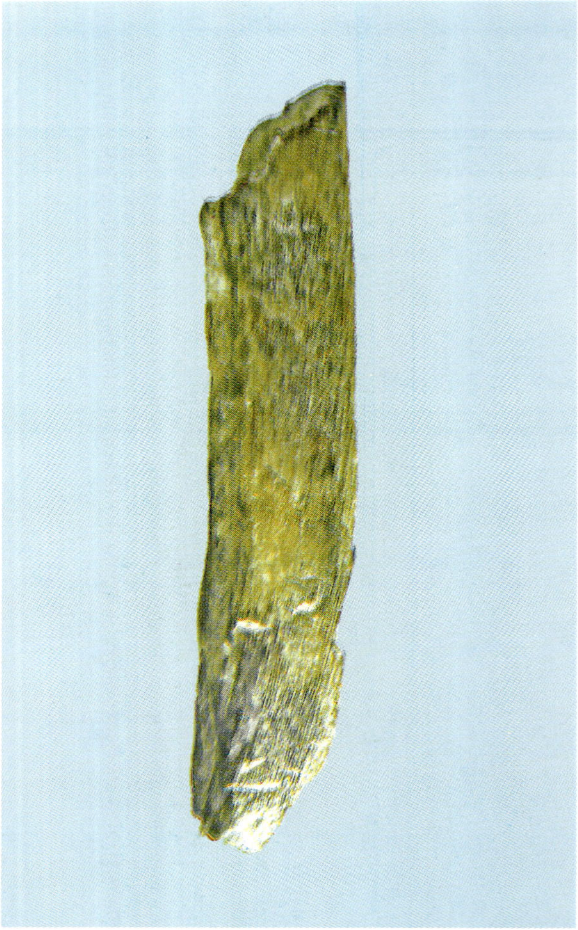

44. The segment of bone (L-5.1 cm), in the round depicts below a human face frontally. The eyes, nose and mouth are well marked.

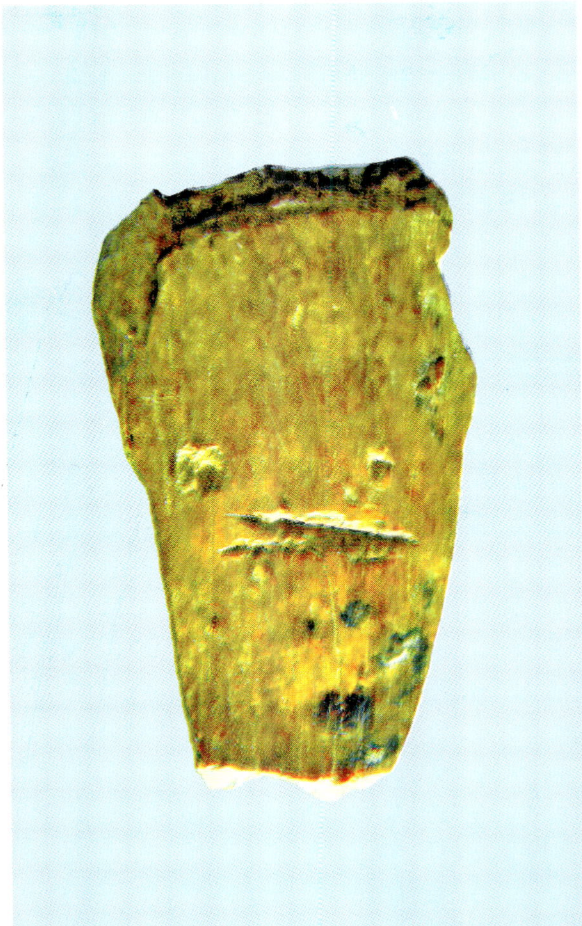

45. A flat segment of bone (2.8 x 1.7 cm), finely cut on all sides. Its lower end is narrower. This specimen is like a mask and depicts the characteristic features of a head full face, showing two holes for two eyes – the proper right one being larger, and two horizontal engravings, either indicating the base of the nose or the mouth. It appears, painting was used to depict other features of the face concerned.

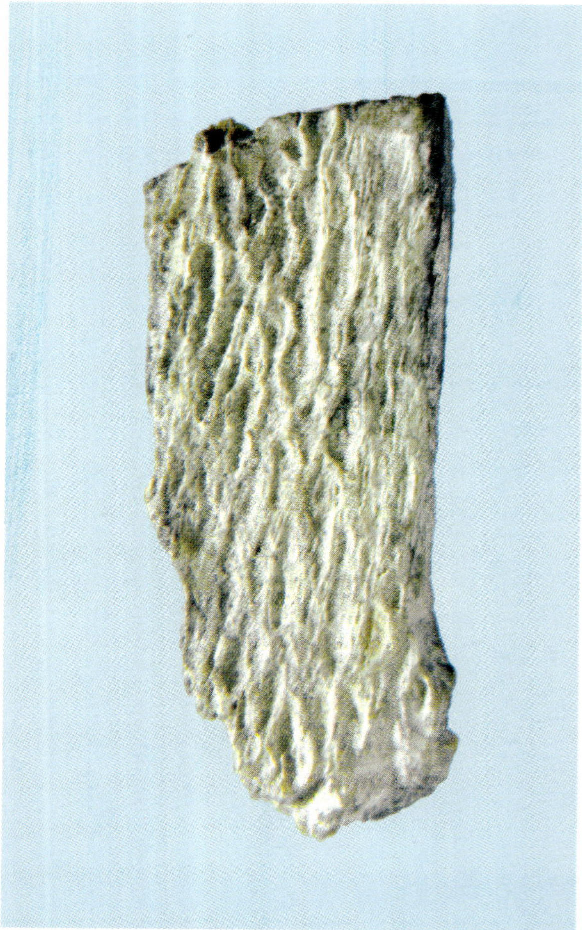

46. Flat thin segment of bone (3.3 x 1.3 cm), showing on its ventral side the profile of a human face to left. Its forehead, nose and mouth are nicely executed along the left border.

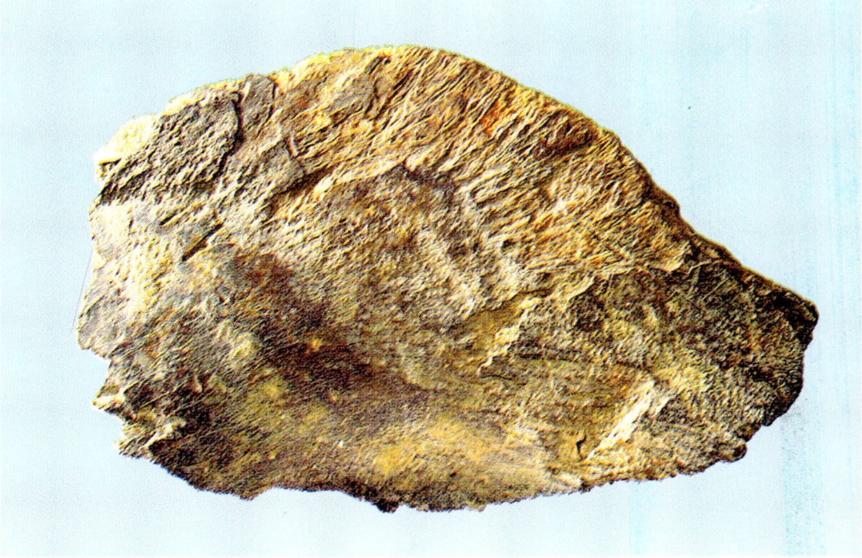

47. Along the left border of the flat segment of bone (8 x 5.5 cm), nose and the lips with mouth are shown well.

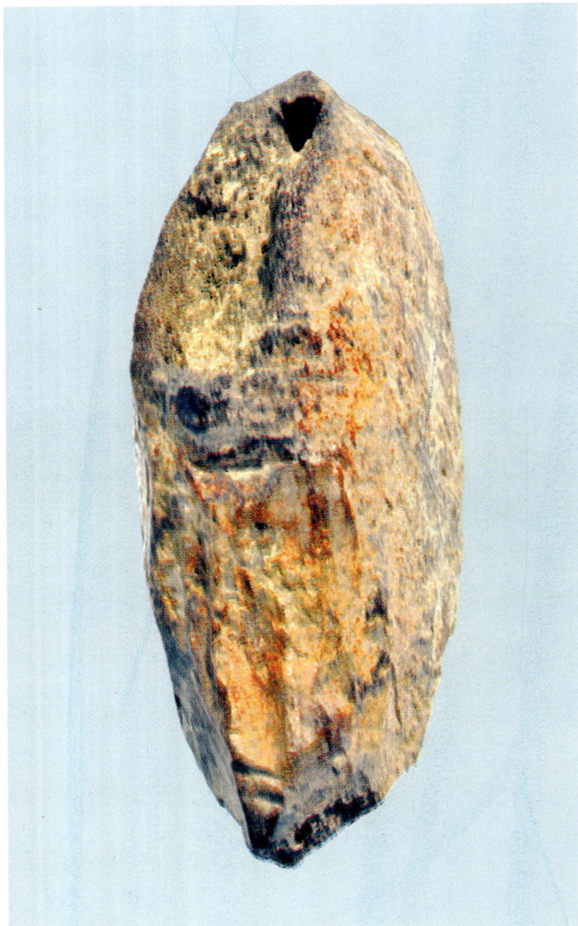

48. It is a small piece of antler (6 x 4 cm). Two short parallel engraved lines mark the lips and mouth below and pin holes, the eyes above. It represents a human face.

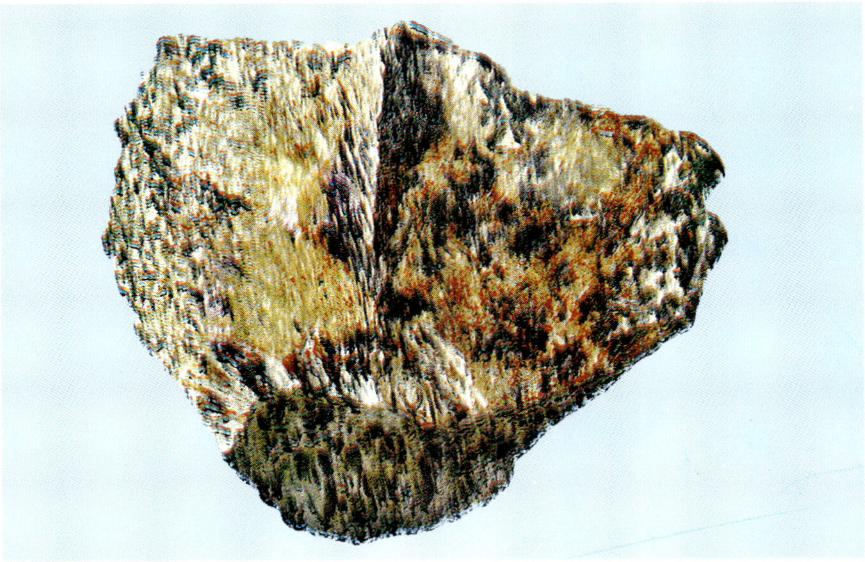

49. The specimen (5 x 5 cm), outlines a human face in profile to right.

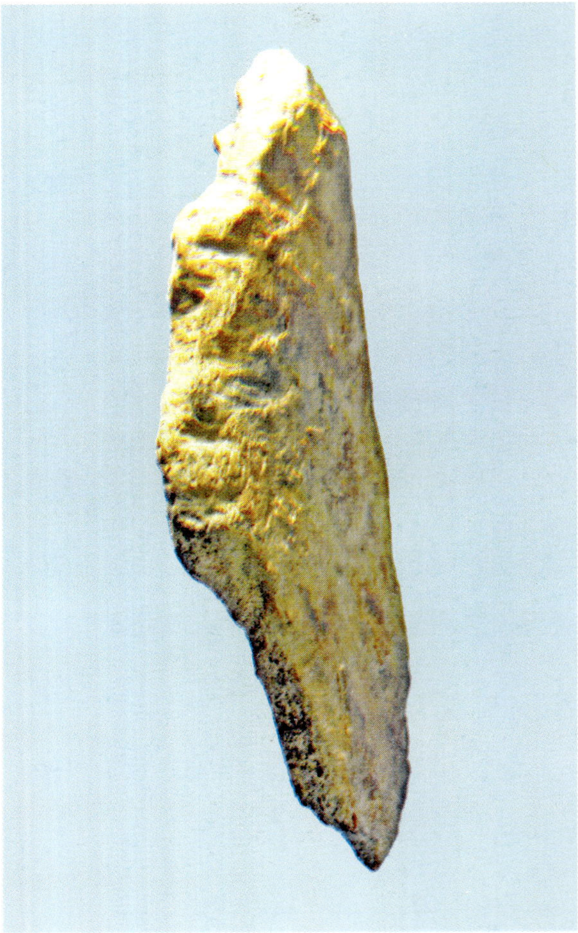

50. Three-fourths frontal view of a human face is carved on this small piece of bone (4 x 1.3 cm), on its dorsal side. While the mouth is nicely carved, its nose is not well defined. Though the round eyes are present, they do not lie at the same horizontal level. Here, the artist's skill to create movement and to bring out and register in the depiction the emotional state of the man represented by the figure is wonderful.

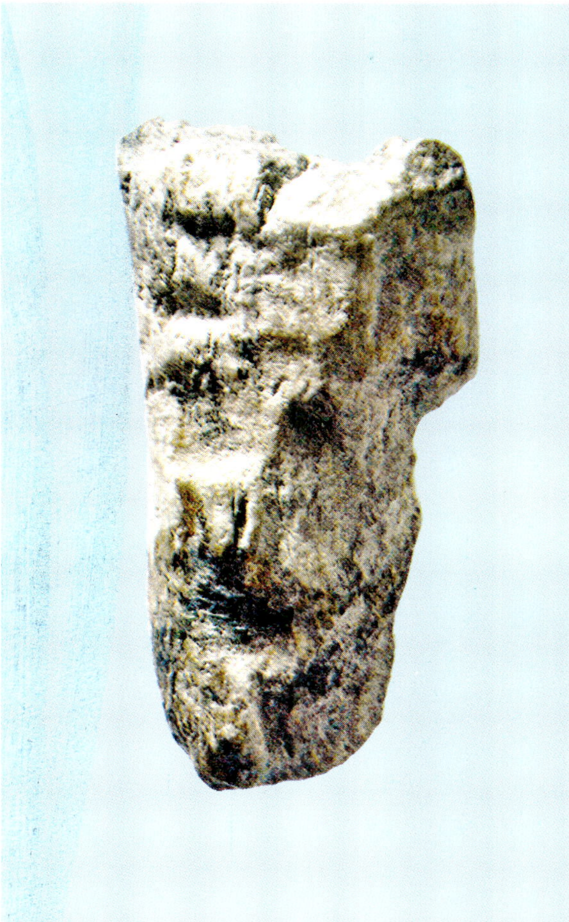

51. It is a very small piece of cleft bone (2.4 x 1.4 cm). Dorsal side is oval. Three dimensional depiction of a male human face with broad forehead, two round eyes by scooping and the mouth by carving is well executed.

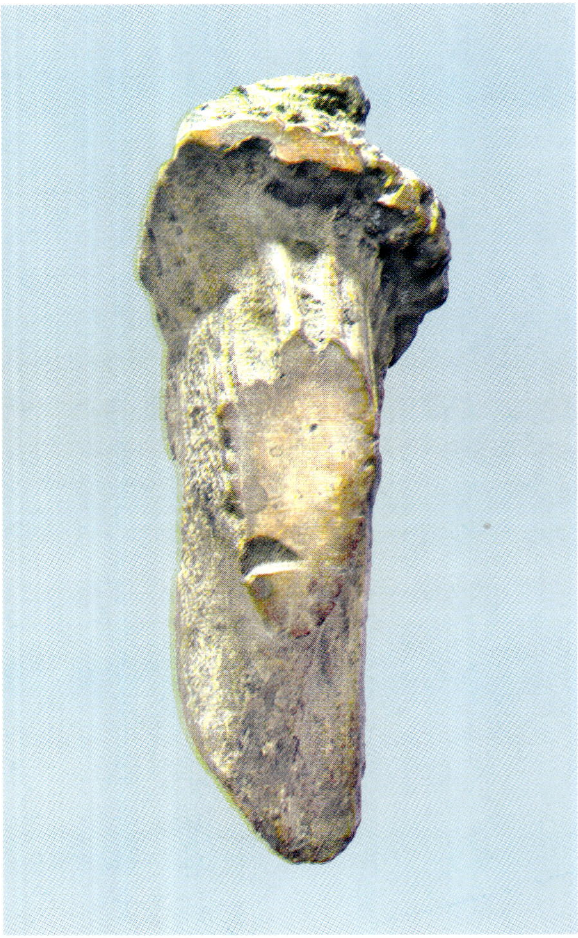

52. It is a piece of antler (L-9.5 cm). A portion is well ground and polished where a human face to left in profile is shown. Open mouth is nicely presented by deep curved engraving. A pinhole above denotes the proper left eye.

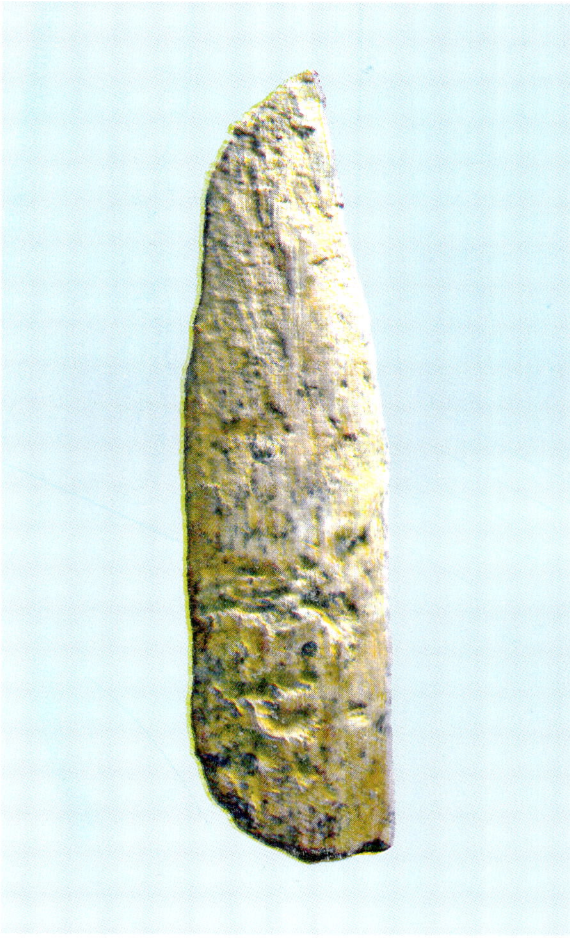

53. It is a cleft piece of bone (8.1 x 2.2 cm). On its curved dorsal side eyes and mouth of a man are shown by engraving frontally. Tapering elongation above is for hanging probably.

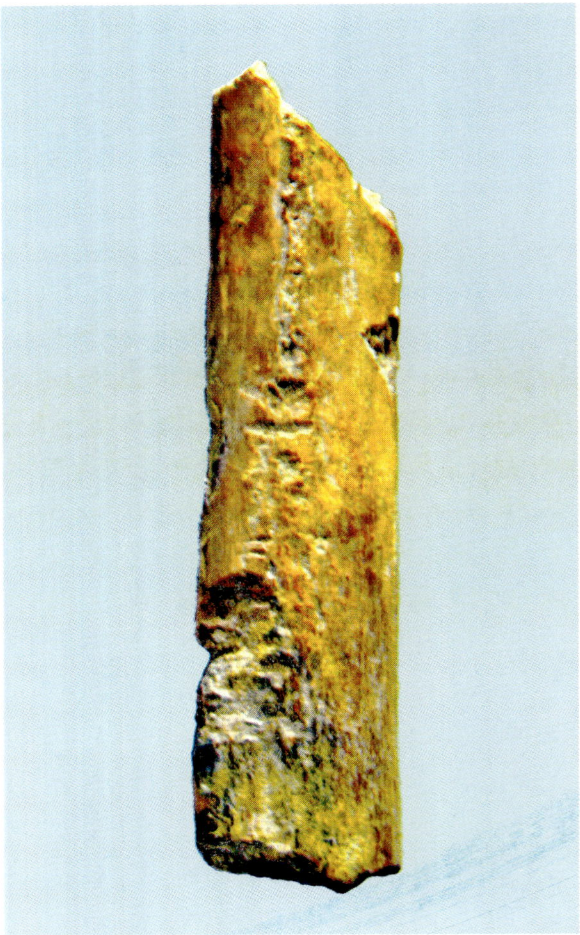

54. It is cylindrical segment of bone (L-3.9 cm), with the engraving of a human face. Here the eye, nose and mouth are partly seen. The same are repeated and extended on the other side. An attempt for carving is also noticeable. Three-dimensional effect and relief may be had from the curvature of bone surface.

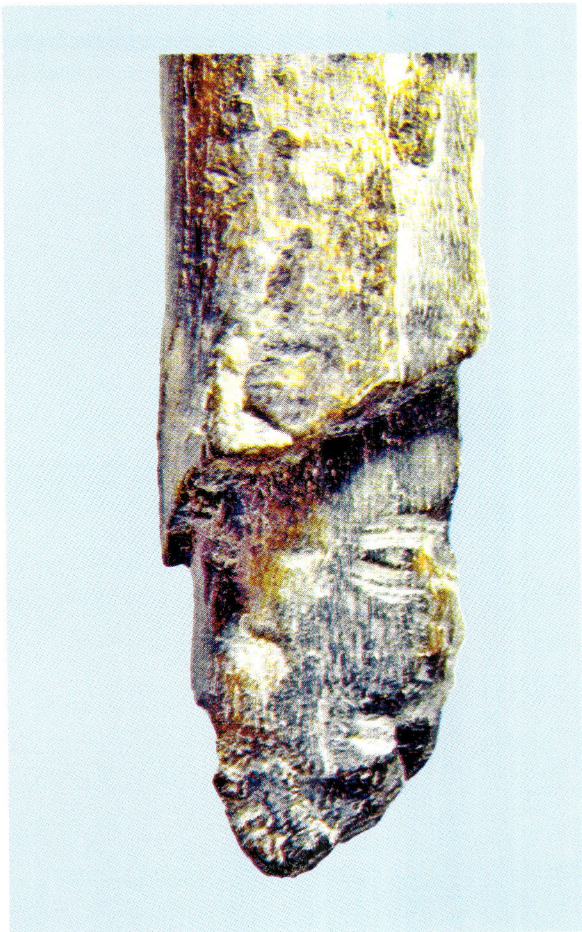

55. Two faces in profile – the larger one to right along the right border and the smaller one to left along the left border, a little below the former, are engraved on the core portion after removing the outer layer of the bone (8.2 x 2.1 cm). In both cases eye, nose, mouth and chin are well marked.

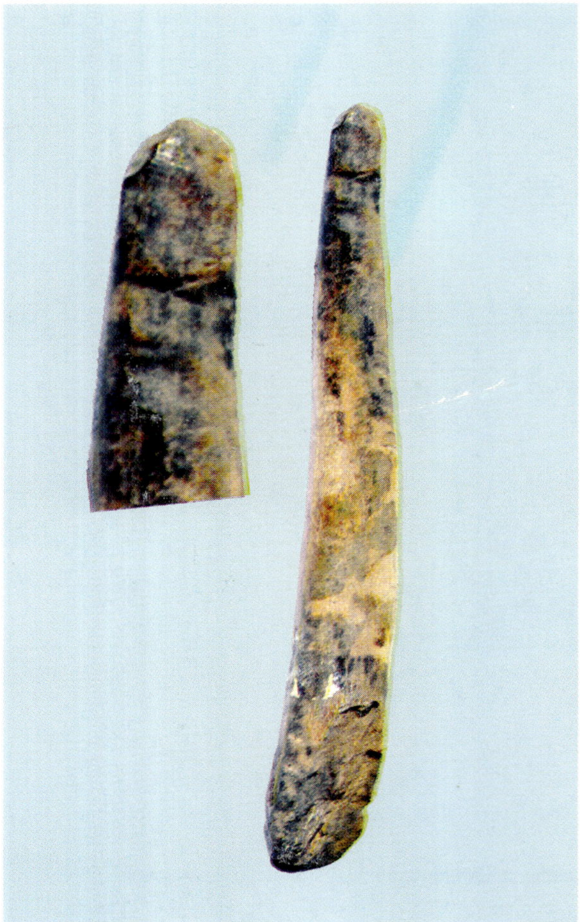

56. It is a piece of antler (L-11 cm). Its upper narrow end is carved in the form of phallus. Below it, is carved a human male face presenting its side-view.

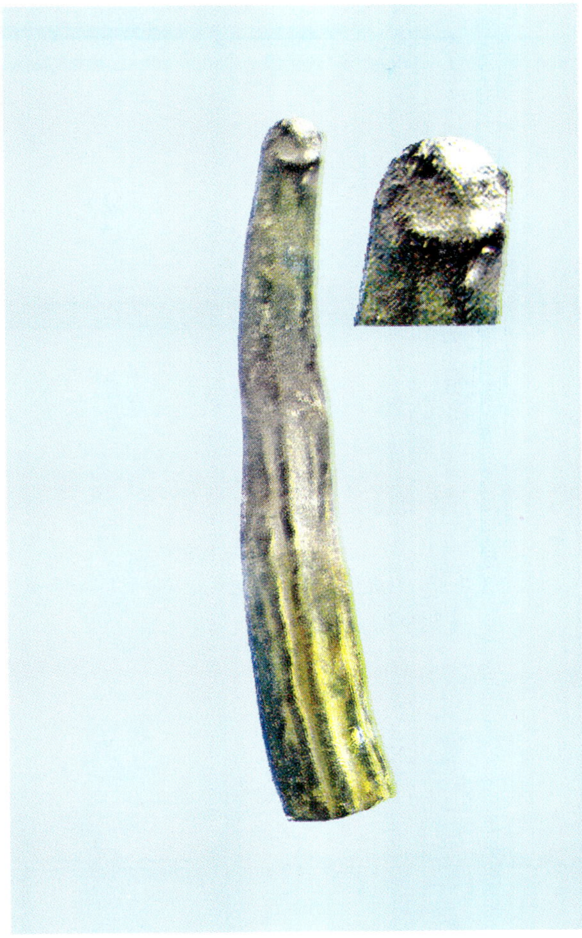

57. It is a piece of antler (L-12.6 cm). The frontal view of a human female face with a round outline is carved on the tip of its narrow upper end. On the back of the head, engraved lines suggest hair.

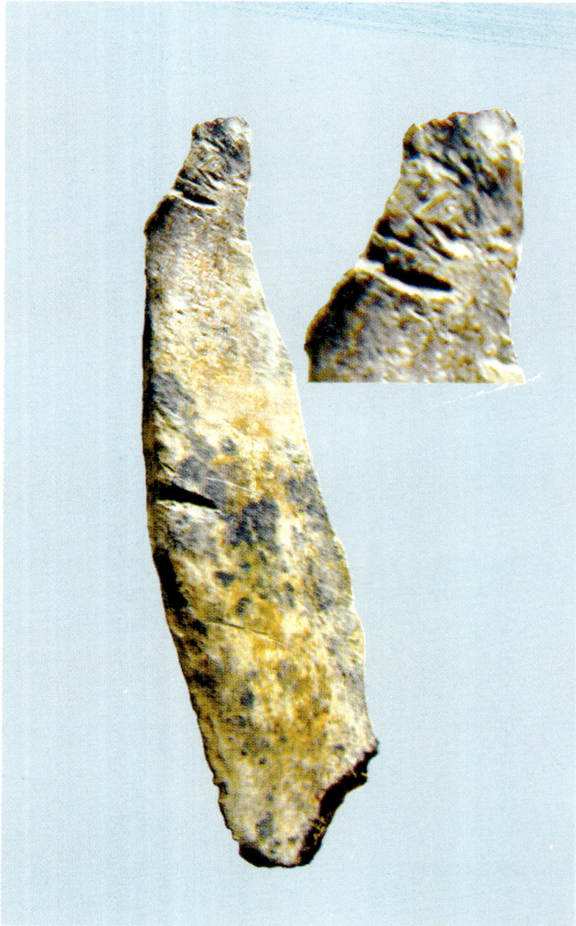

58. It is a small flat piece of bone (7.5 x 1.8 cm), with the depiction of a human face above. Three-fourths frontal view of a human face with wide open mouth, eye and nose is engraved. The head is tilted to right.

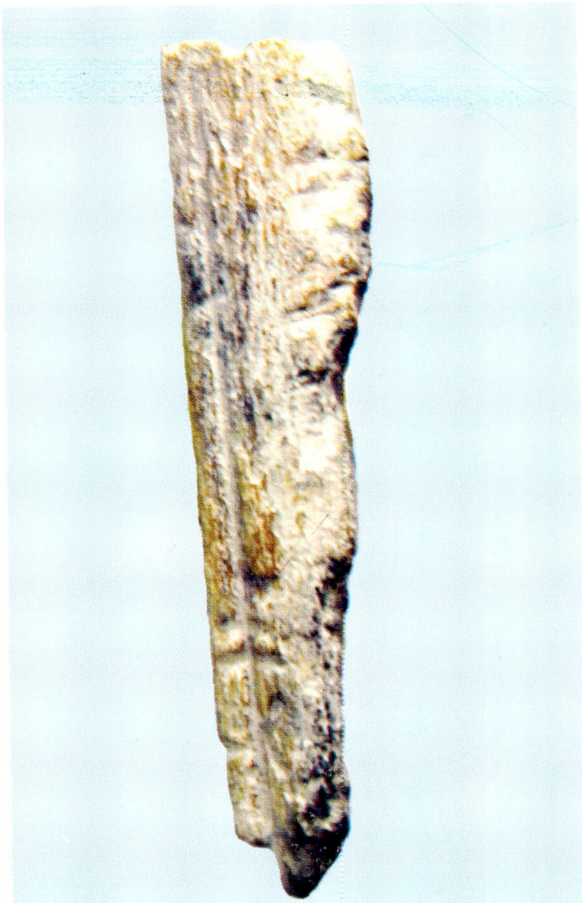

59. The small piece of bone (5 x 1.5 cm), at its upper broad end shows the side view of a human face with forehead, eye, nose and mouth. Profiles of two faces side-by-side are engraved at its narrow end below.

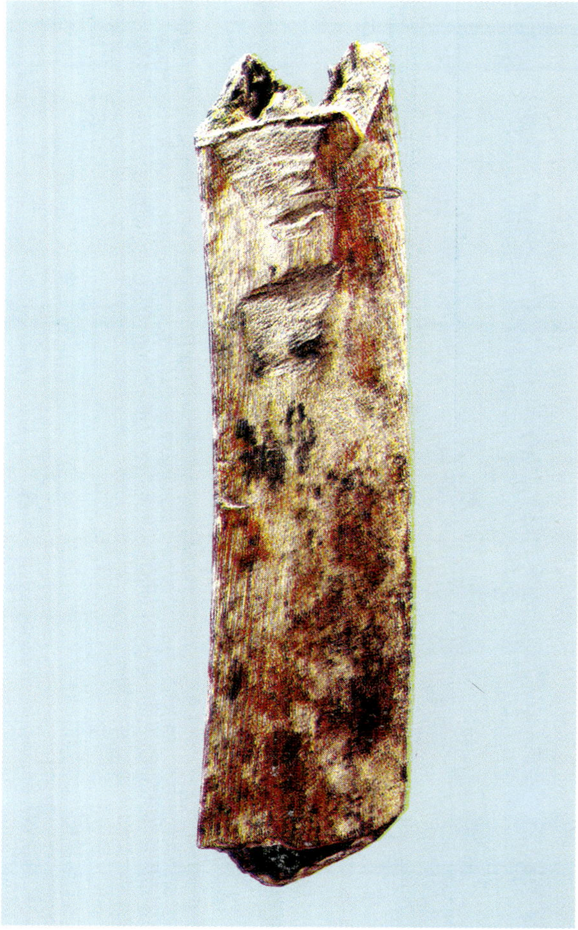

60. It is a small flat piece of bone (6.4 x 1.6 cm). A human face is depicted above. Its eyes, open mouth and heavy lower jaw are clearly shown. The human being seems to be robust and he looks upwards.

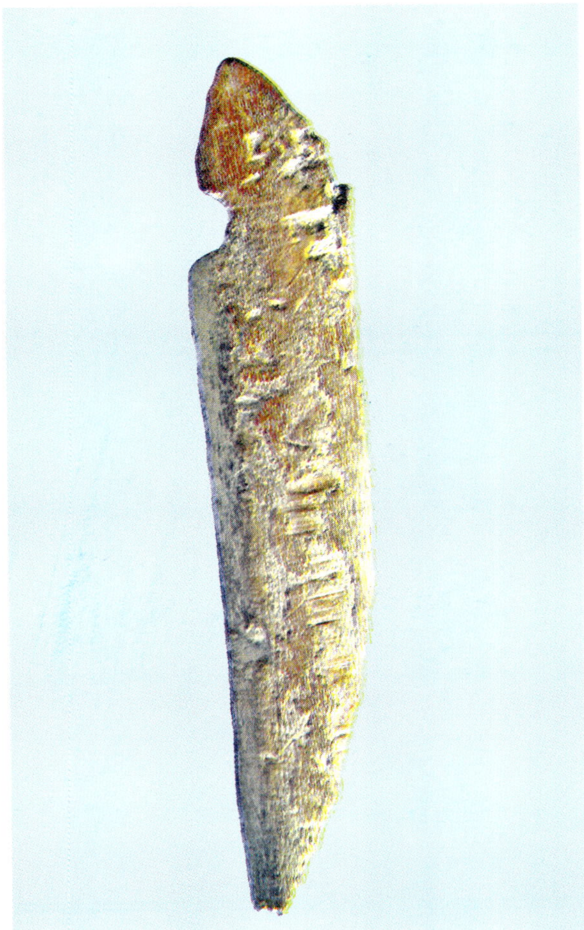

61. It is a cleft and fractured piece of bone (5.3 x 1 cm). The head is conical. Two round eyes, mouth and the neck are shown. Several horizontal cut-marks are seen below.

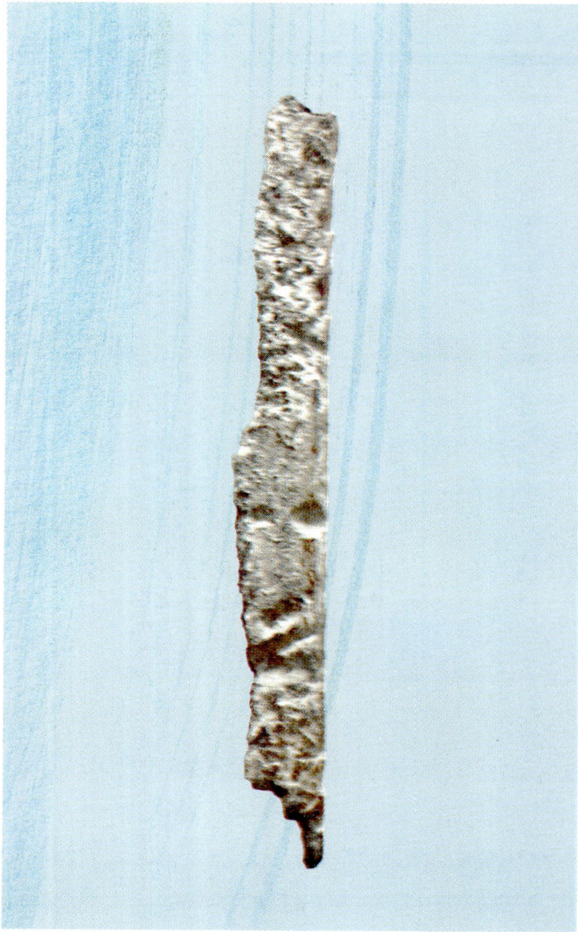

62. A fiercely looking face is depicted at the lower middle portion of the cleft bone (8 x 1 cm). Its proper left round eye is larger than the proper right. The lips are engraved. The face is a little turned to proper right as it appears from the depiction.

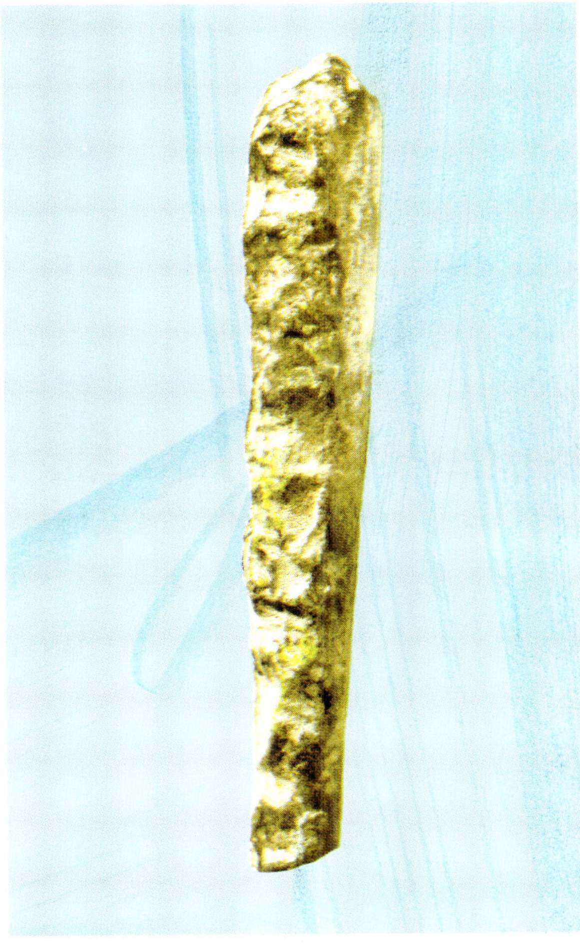

63. Three faces are carved on the thick section in between the dorsal and the ventral sides of the specimen (4.8 x 1.4 cm), and are arranged one below the other. While the face above gives the full frontal view, the two below are a little turned to proper right.

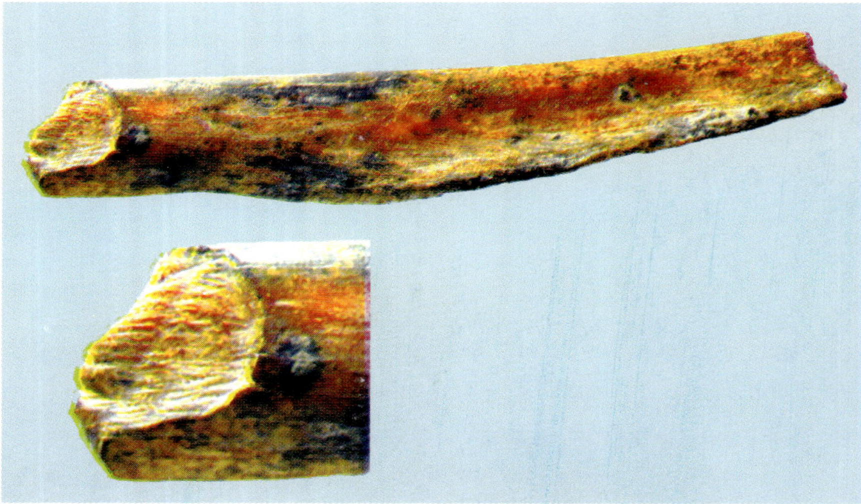

64. A flake is detached from the left end of bone (8.7 x 1.5 cm), and the face of a female in profile to left is carved nice. The figure is in lying posture.

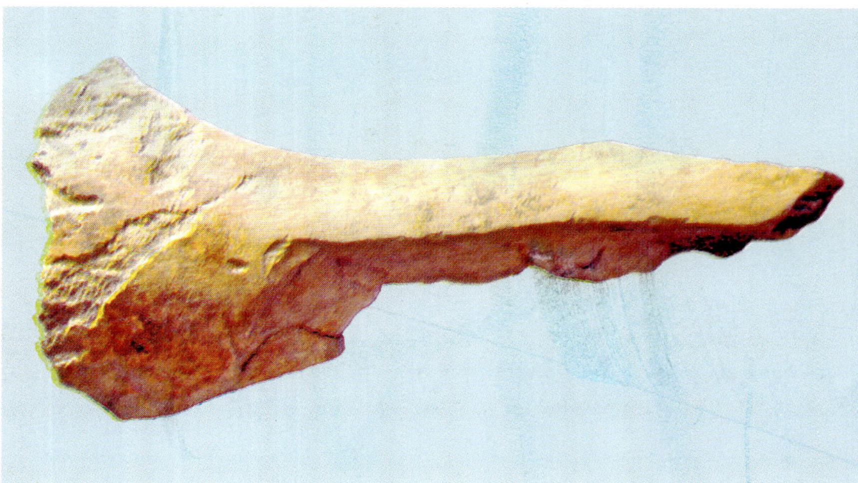

65. On the flat left end of a cleft and fractured bone (9.5 x 5 cm), a face probably representing a female face in profile to left is engraved.

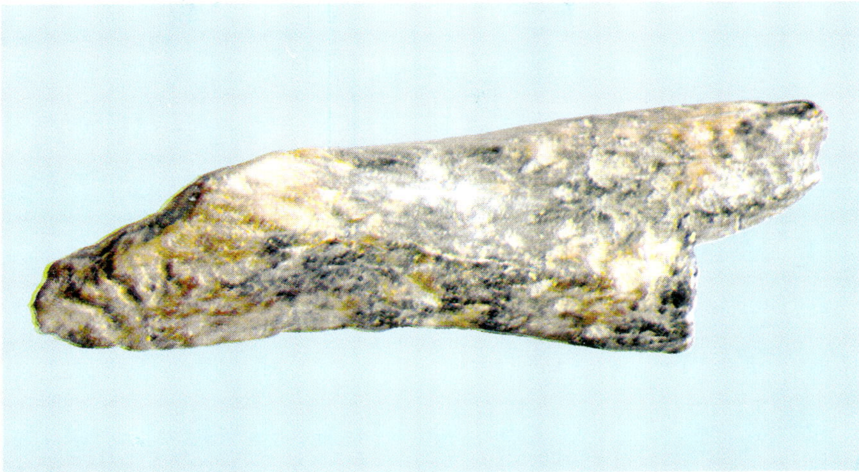

66. Broad nose, mouth and heavy chin of the proper left half of a human face are portrayed on the left border of the cleft bone (5.5 x 1.7 cm). Posture of the motif suggests lying.

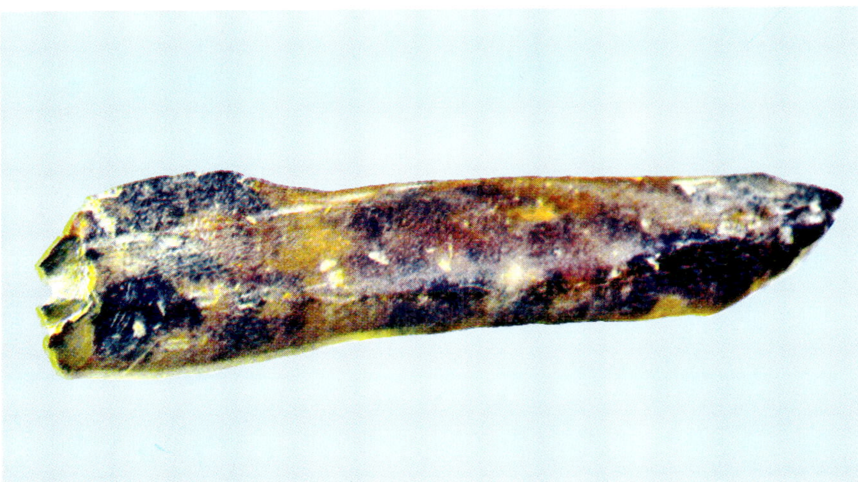

67. The head of a human figure to left is seen in lying posture. Its mouth, chin and cranium are shown clearly along the left border of the specimen (L-4.7 cm).

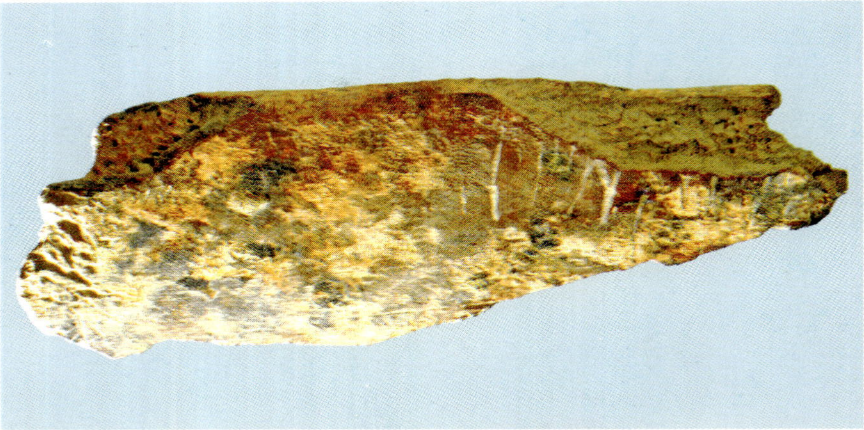

68. A face in profile to left is seen in lying posture. Its mouth, lips, chin are well executed on the left border of the cleft and fractured piece of bone (8 x 3 cm).

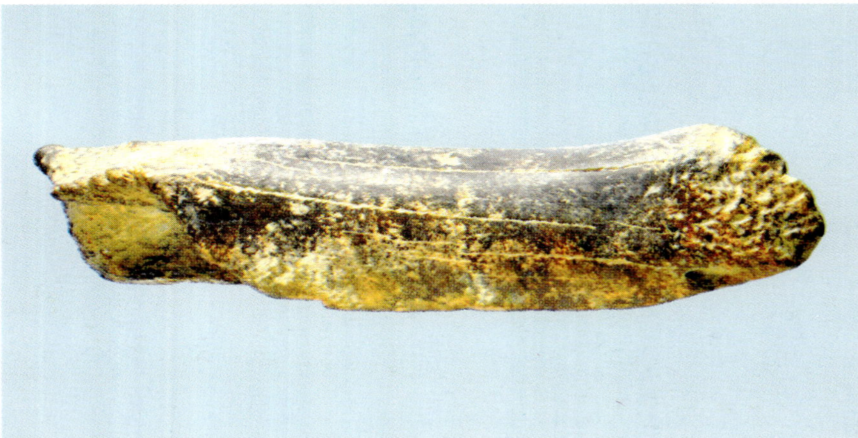

69. A human face in profile to right is executed on the right border of the bone (11.2 x 2 cm). Thick lips, nose and round eyes are seen. Innumerable marks of pecking may stand either for decoration or for indication of ailment like pox. Black paint is noticeable on the bone.

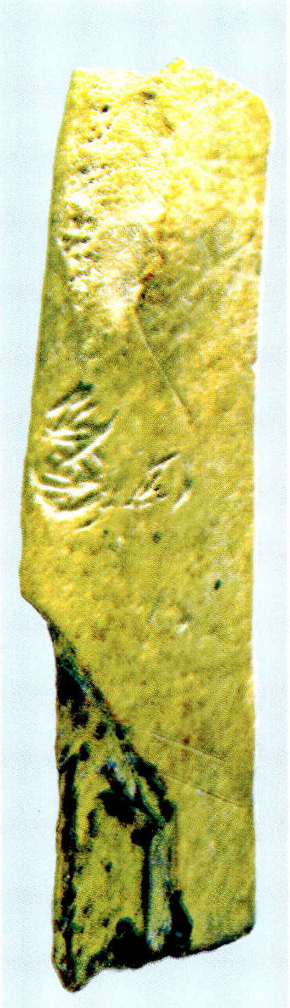

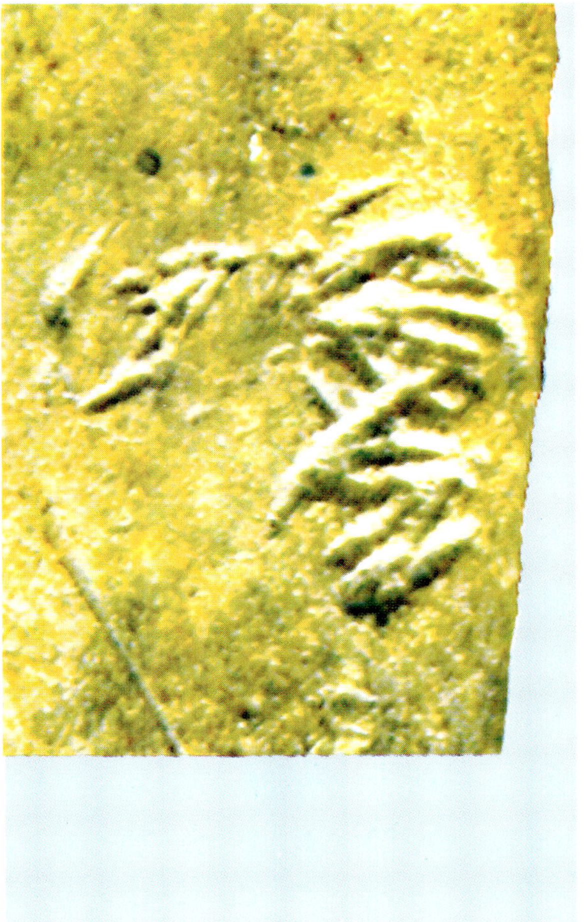

70. While the upper end of this specimen (5 x 1.7 cm), is ground and a human face is engraved in profile to left, the middle portion is engraved deep with a strange head in profile. But the engraving in the middle appears to resemble a human head in profile to left with long pointed nose, two lips with protruding chin, two eyes and forehead and it is to be seen by holding the specimen upside down, i.e., two faces are portrayed in opposite direction.

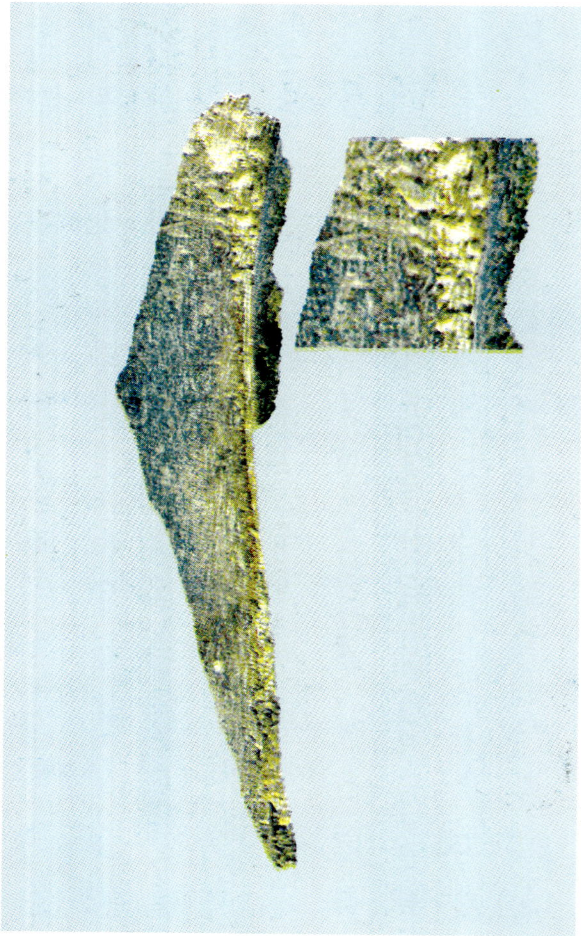

71. The specimen (7.3 x 1.7 cm), is black and it represents the frontal view of a face of a fiercely strange being with round eyes and mouth. It seems to be the imaginary depiction of a devil by the artist.

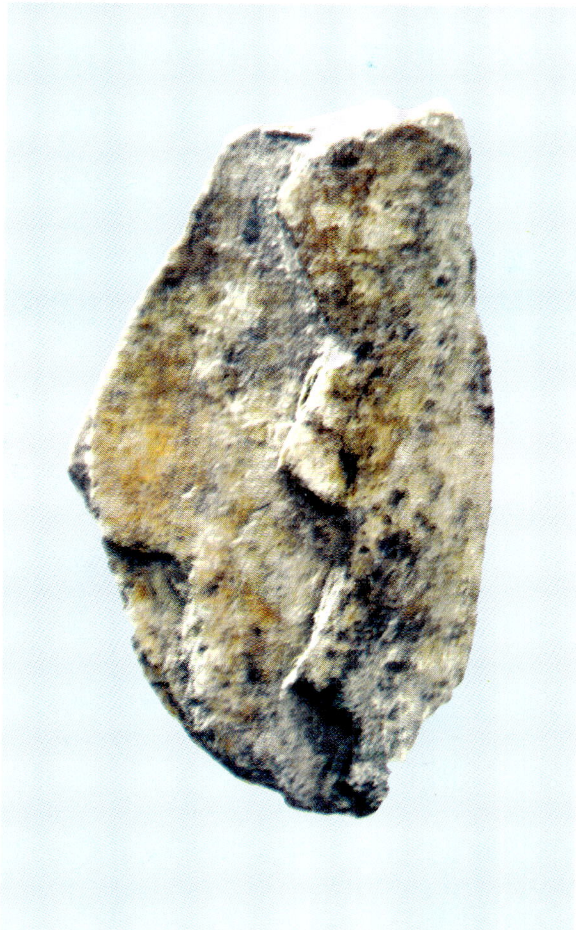

72. The specimen (3.7 x 2.1 cm), is a fine piece of carving. Probably a female in profile to left is carved in low relief. Head, breast and the portion below waist are indicated.

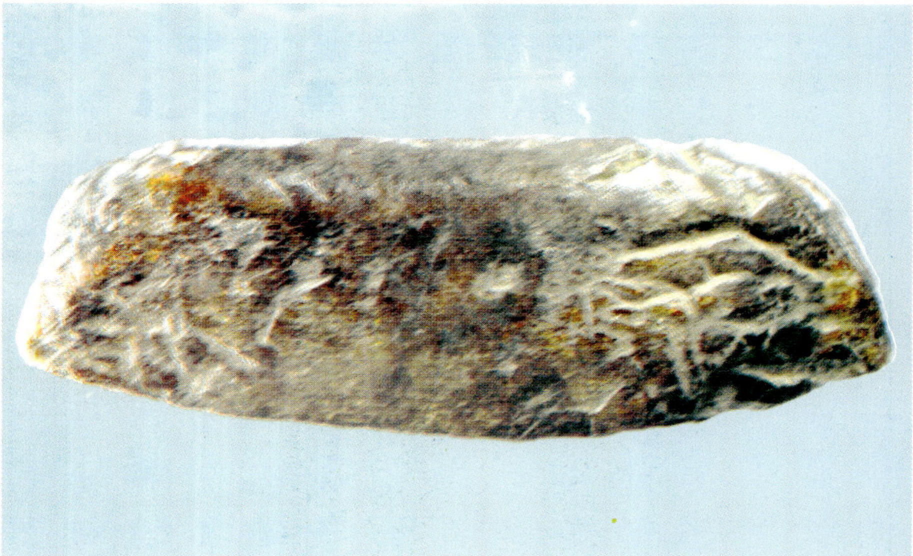

73. On this thick ground piece of bone (5 x 1.7 cm), two motifs are engraved. On left, the face of a human-like being is engraved in formal profile to right, with wide open mouth, nose, forehead and a small circular eye. On right the head of some animal is engraved in profile to right. Animal figures had been painted in black before engravings and traces of black paint are noticeable on the specimen. From the depiction, it appears that the bestial being on left is in an attempt to chase the animal on right, which tries to run away.

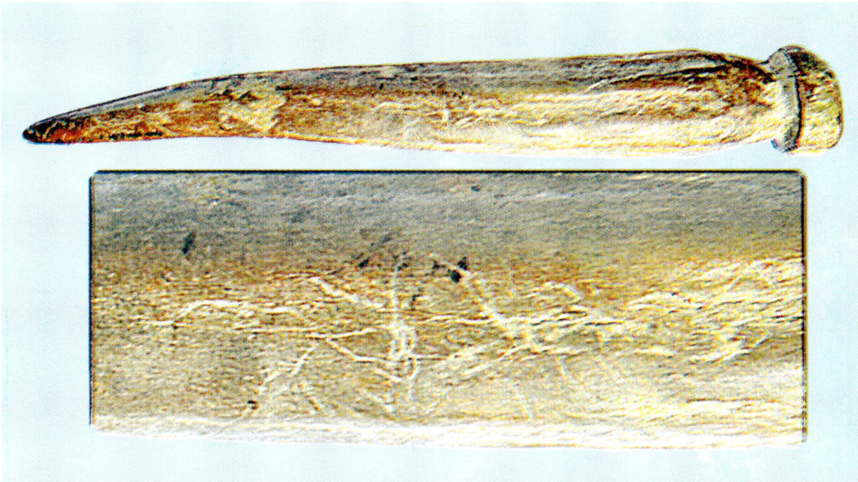

74. It is a dagger made of antler (L-10.5 cm). On the middle of this specimen horned animals are engraved. Two animals are clearly seen. They are in formal profile facing each other.

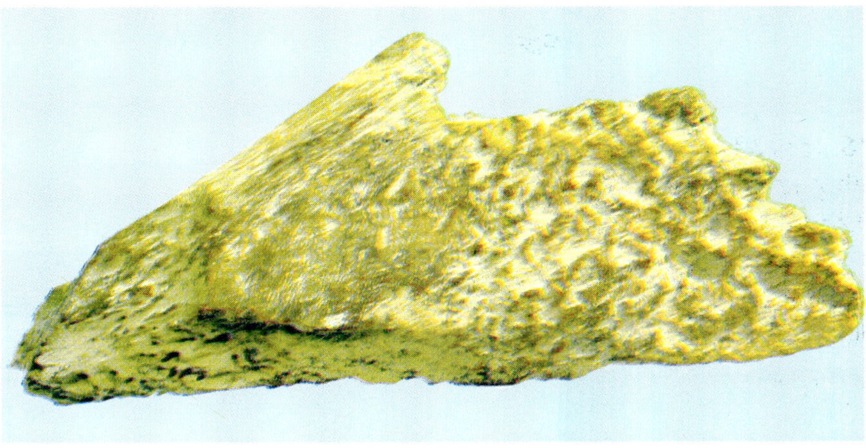

75. The segment of bone (6 x 3.7 cm), portrays an animal lying, as if taking rest after mid-day meal, with its body coiled and the head resting on the ground to right. The mouth, nose and eye-socket are nicely executed by the techniques of engraving and pecking. The beast is shown in formal profile. Possibly it represents a carnivorous animal.

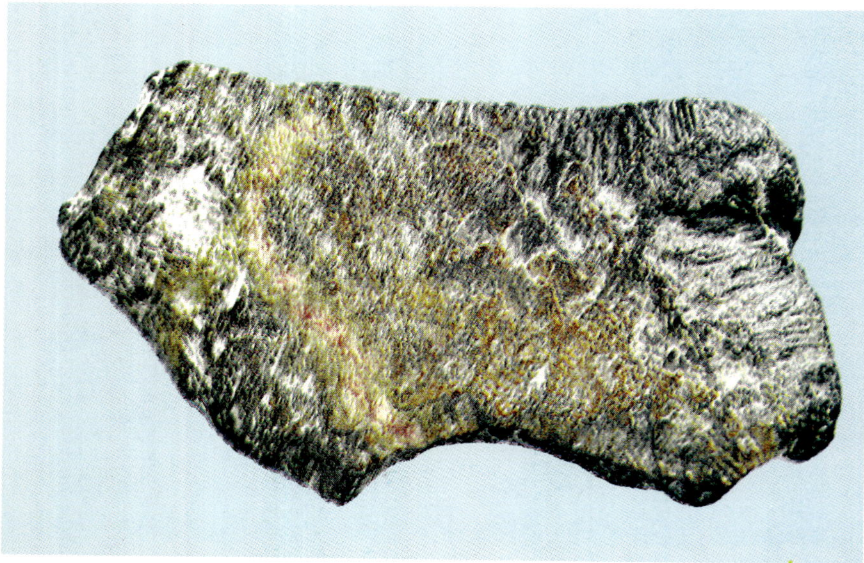

76. It is a thin piece of bone (4.9 x 2.6 cm), with sharp sides on left and above. It could be used as a blade. However, on right the side-view of the face of a beast, like gorilla, is seen. The cranium, two round eyes above and a round mouth below and the curved border representing the outline of nose are important to take note of. Vertical engraved lines may be taken to stand for hair on the body.

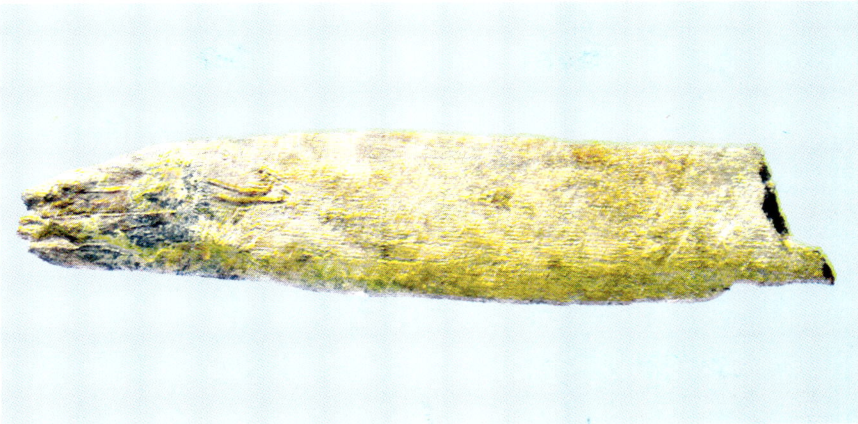

77. On the dorsal side of the cleft bone (8.7 x 1.9 cm), the forepart of a being to left is executed in formal profile. The head is separated by deeply engraved curved lines. One eye, nose, lips and chin are well defined. The figure has been fashioned by slitting, scooping and engraving.

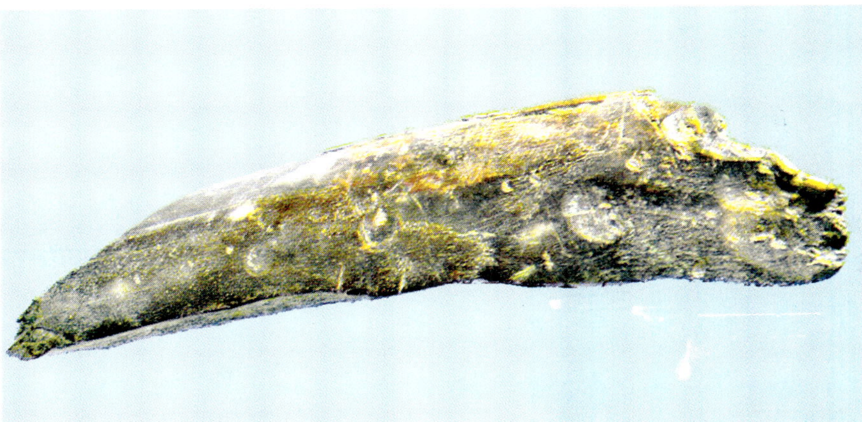

78. The cleft bone (8.1 x 2.4 cm), representing the forepart of a beast to right in formal profile. The mouth is well fashioned as also the nose and forehead, by using the techniques of flaking and engraving. It appears, the beast concerned stands for a carnivore.

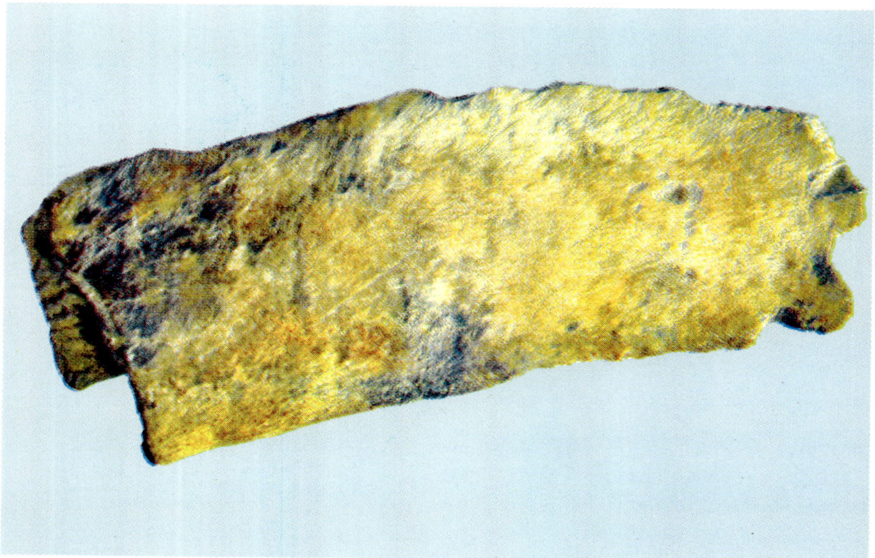

79. The flat segment of rib (6.7 x 2.5 cm), presenting the formal profile of a yawning face of some animal. A small longish hole surrounded by punctured design to the left of the nose marks the eye. Traces of daubing in black colour still persist at places. It may represent a rhino.

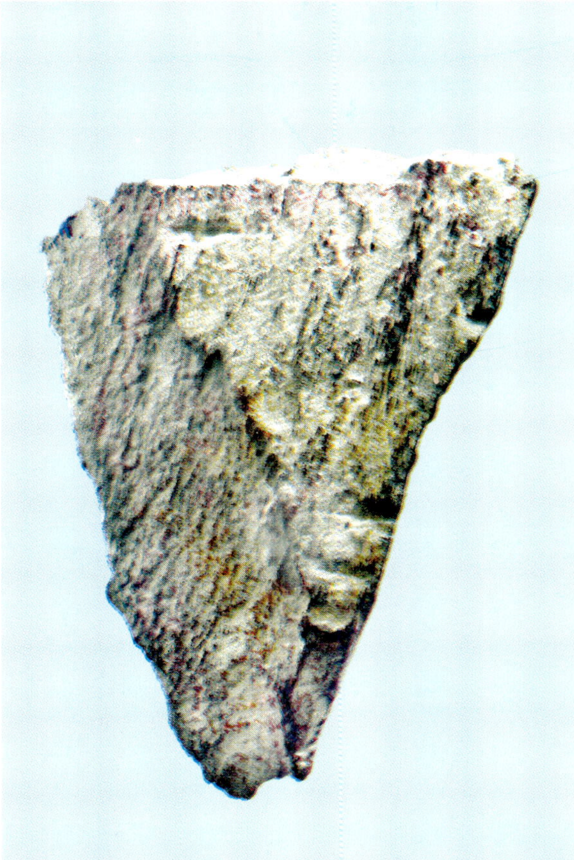

80. It is a hand-axe-like specimen (9.6 x 6.5 cm), with sharp edge on left border and below. Might be, it was used to cut things and grub edible roots. However, on the dorsal side, the head of an animal is depicted full face with the marks of two eyes and nose, lips and chin with short parallel horizontal engravings bellow.

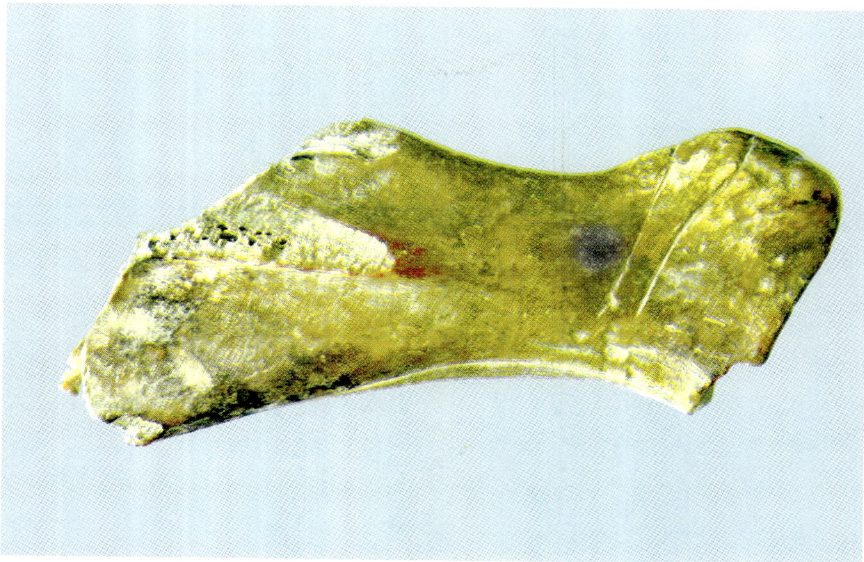

81. The specimen (6.5 x 2.4 cm), is cut in the shape of an animal head to left in profile. While the neck is marked by two parallel and curved engraved lines a little before the edge on right, the mouth and nose are indicated by flaking on the left border. Traces of paint indicating the eye is still noticeable. The outline prompts us to take it for the head of a dog-like animal.

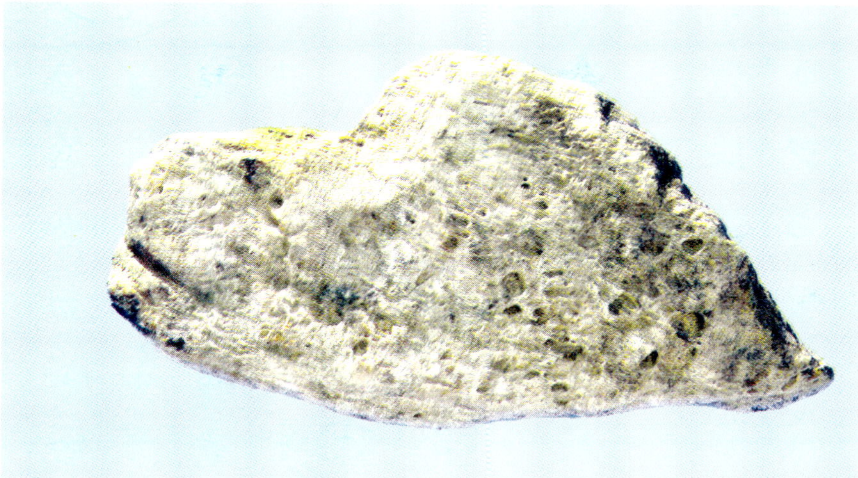

82. The segment of a flat bone (5.5 x 2.9 cm), gives on its ventral side the side-view of a head that resembles that of a monkey. The forehead, nose and mouth are well indicated. The mouth has been fashioned by engraving and the nose and forehead exist forming an obtuse angle. The side opposite to the face ends in a point.

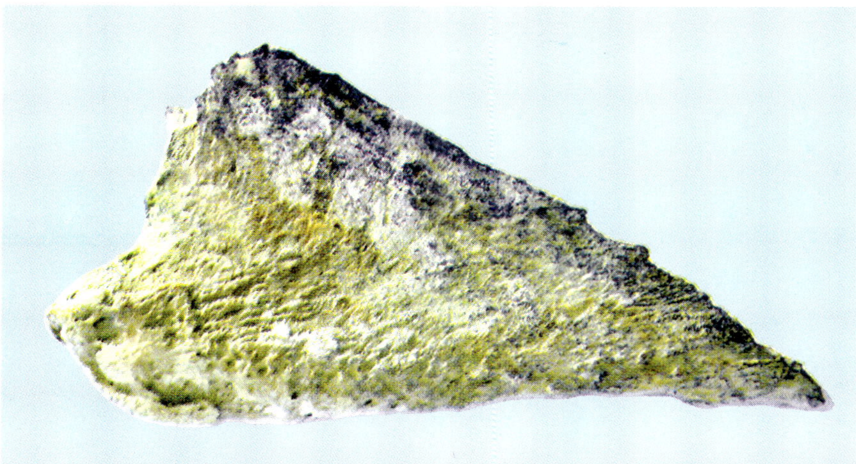

83. The segment (6.3 x 3.5 cm), representing the forepart of the face of a hyena or dog-like animal to left in profile. Its nose and mouth are nicely shown by engraving and carving.

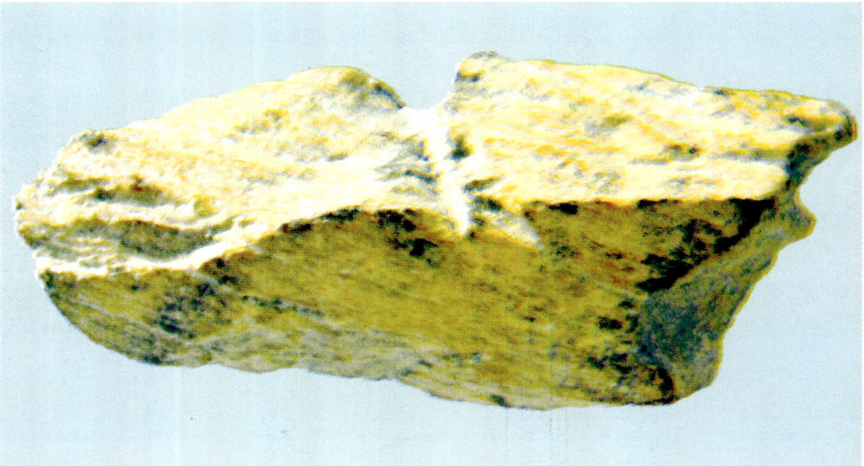

84. Profile of the forepart of what appears to be the head of a horse-like animal, is carved on the dorsal side of this small segment of bone (2.6 x 1.2 cm). The features of the face have been brought out by engraving. The notch on the bridge of the nose was possibly meant for binding it to a rope.

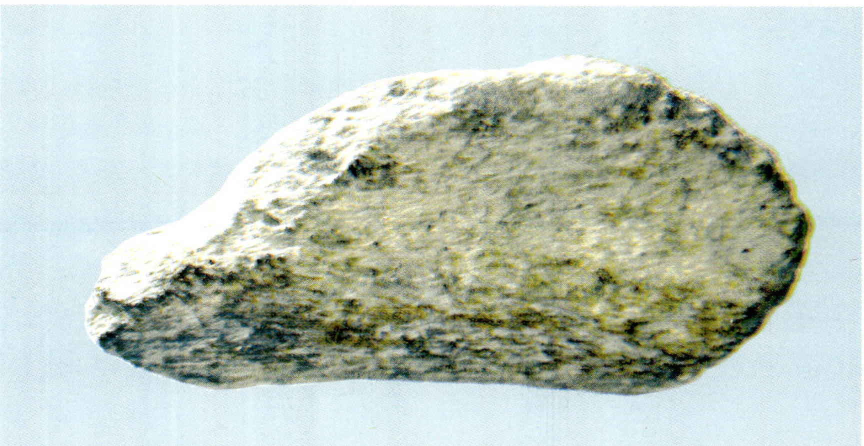

85. The segment (3.2 x 1.8 cm), represents the head of some animal to left in profile. The cranium, nose and mouth are shown by carving.

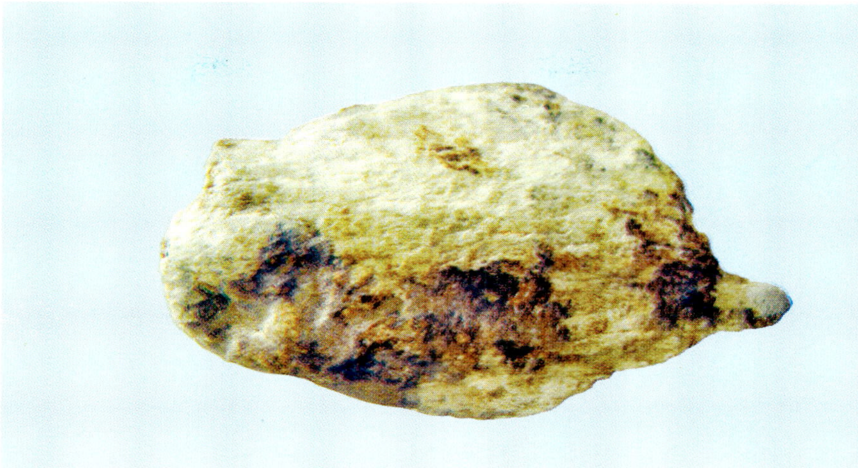

86. The specimen (3.4 x 2 cm), is almost round depicting the profile of an animal head to left. The mouth is nicely carved. It appears, paint was used to show the eye and ear etc. A tenon on right is retained possibly to bind it to a thread or to fix it to the remaining part of the body.

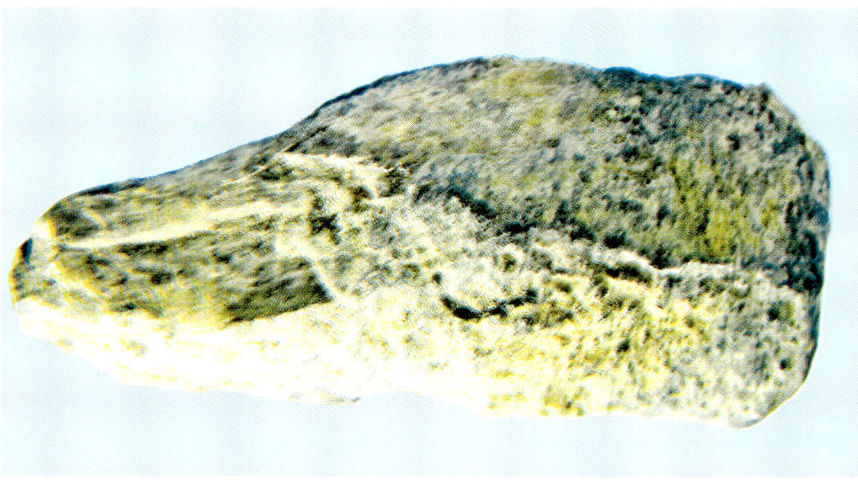

87. The specimen (3.3 x 1.7 cm), represents a head of some strange animal with a flat cranium, very long and flat nose, a cheek and a mouth to left. It is nicely carved.

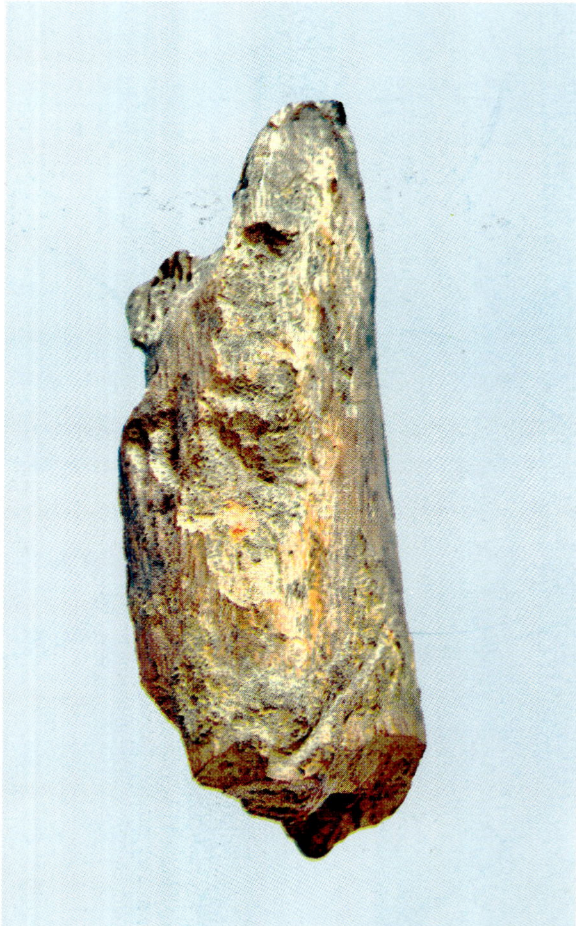

88. It is a small cylindrical piece of bone (L-4 cm), fractured above. On it is depicted naturalistically and nicely the head of a fox-like animal with two round eyes above and a slanting engraved line dividing the jaws below.

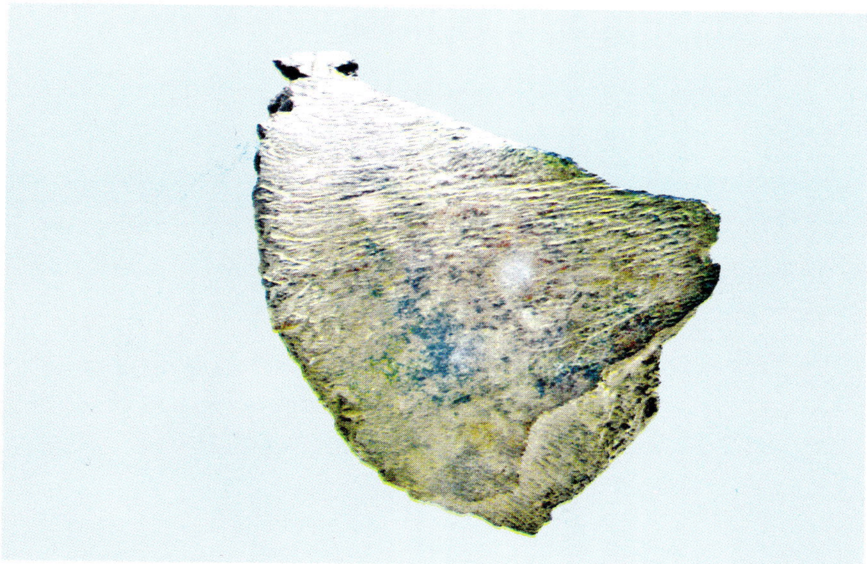

89. This specimen (14 x 11 cm), is cut in the form of a head of a beast, probably a bear, to right in profile. A small head of a beast is seen above. If seen from the other side the presence of the small head seems to be the part of a very big animal having long hair that is hinted at by the engraved lines coming down from the back.

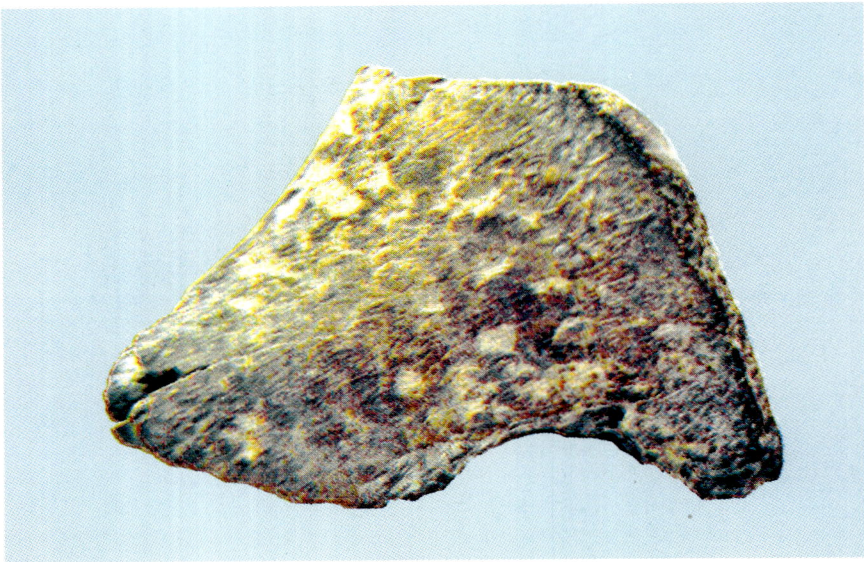

90. The specimen (3 x 3 cm), is cut in the form of an animal head in profile to left. Marks of pecking are noticeable all over the face.

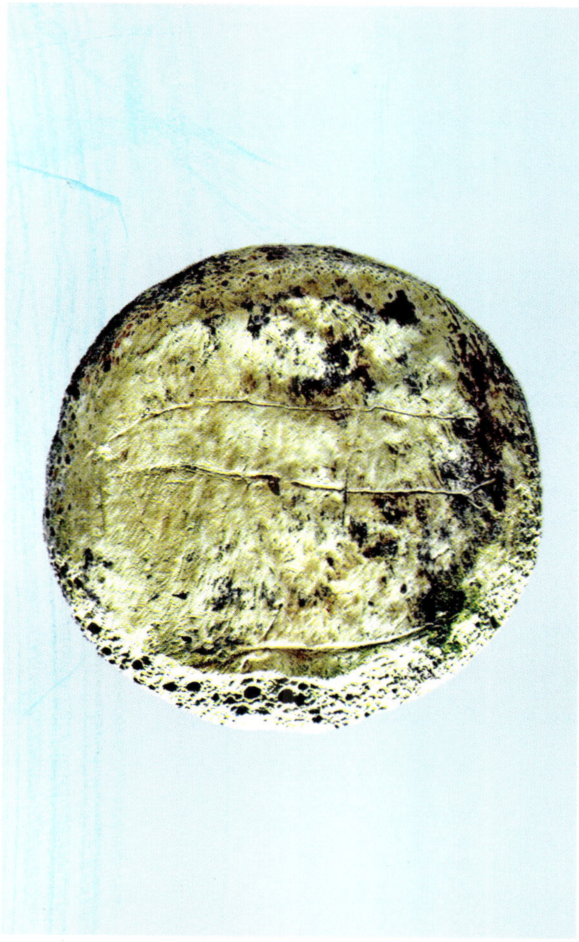

91. The specimen (D- 5.8 cm), probably depicts the engraving of an aquatic being to the left.

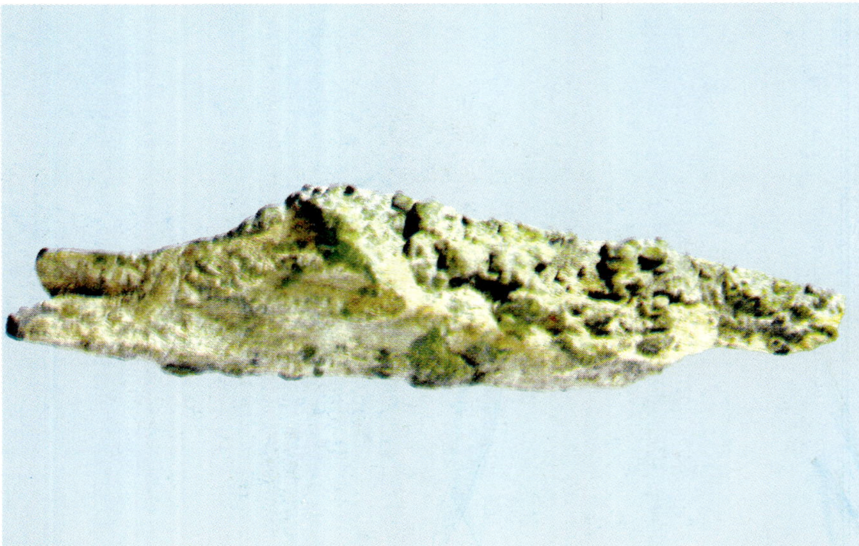

92. The segment of bone (6.7 x 1.6 cm), representing either an aquatic reptile or fish to left. Its forepart is nicely carved.

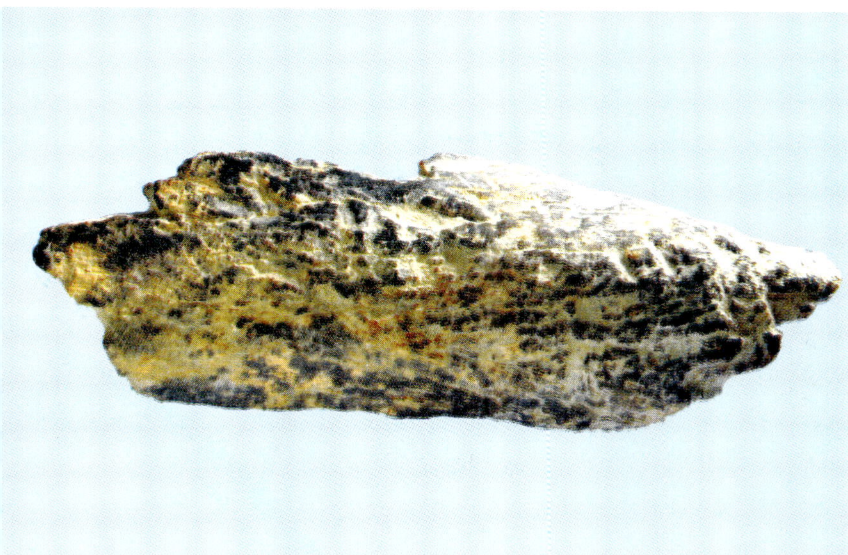

)3. The specimen (7 x 2.5 cm), appears to represent a fish. Engravings on the back probably signify scale. Dorsal fin and tail in seem to be indicated.

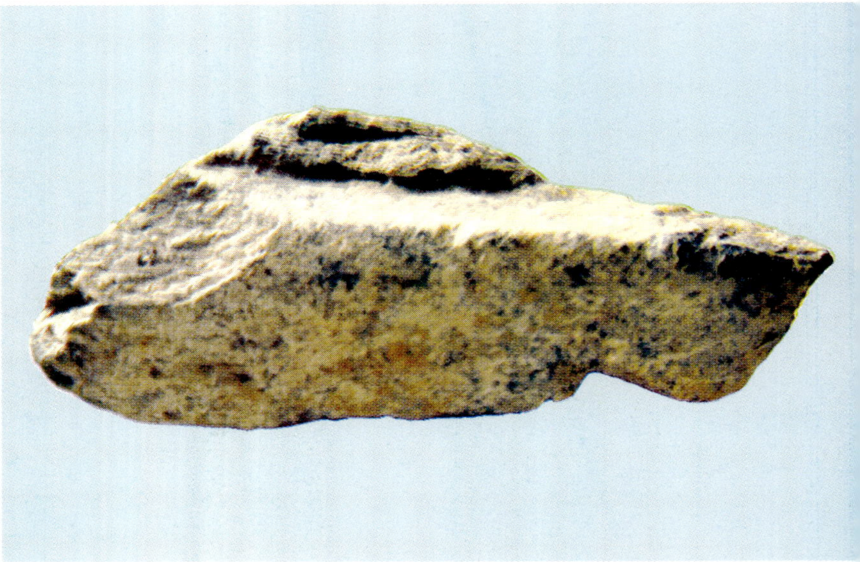

94. This specimen (4.5 x 2 cm), represents a fish in profile to left
Its mouth is on left. Its dorsal fin and caudal fin are present.

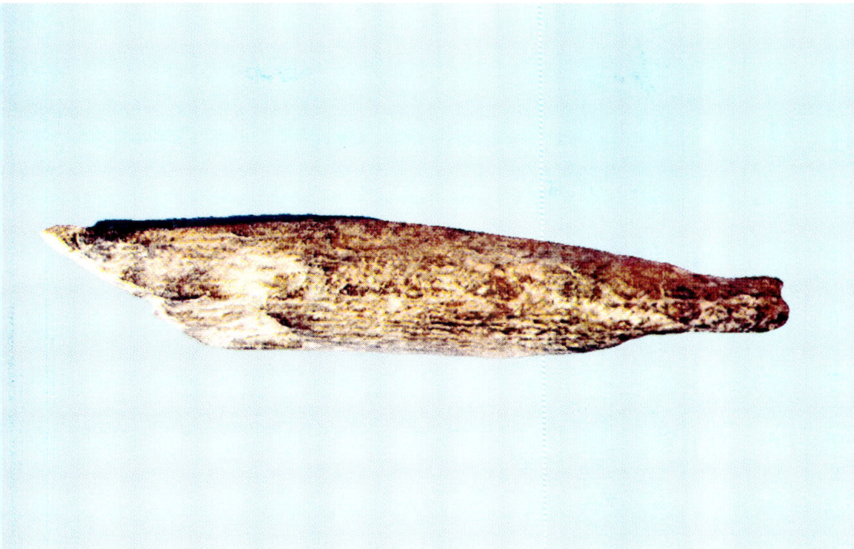

95. It represents a fish and is shown in profile to left. Its tail fin is clearly shown on right. Traces of black paintings are seen all over. The example measures 8.5 x 1.6 cm.

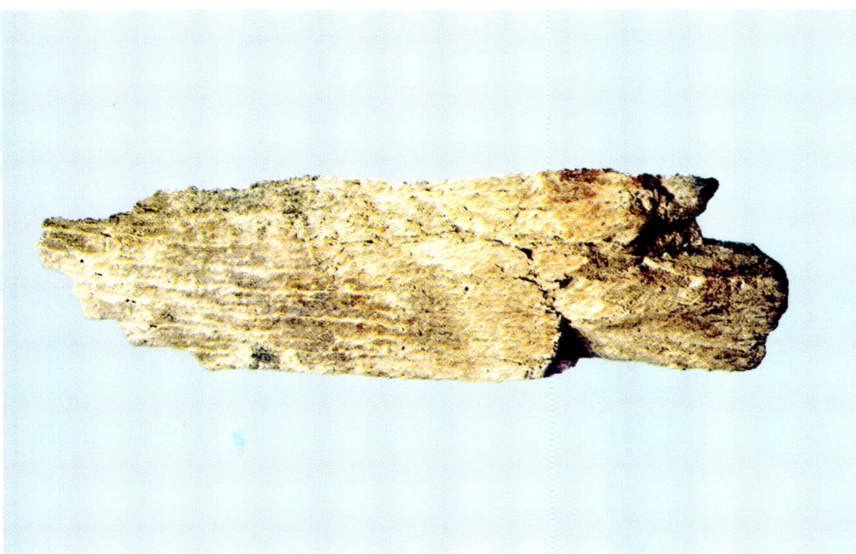

96. The specimen (8.5 x 2.2 cm), represents an aquatic being, probably a fish. Its dorsal fin and tail fin are shown on right.

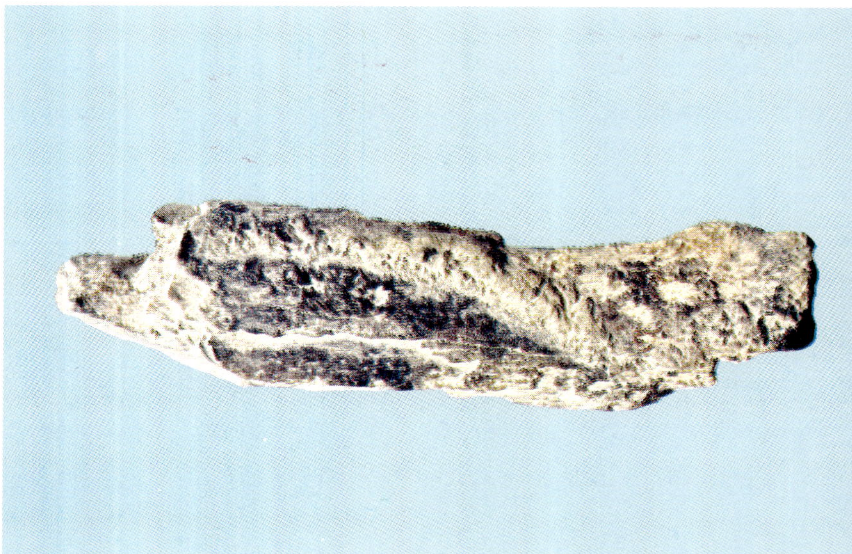

97. This bone (8.6 x 2.4 cm), represents a fish. Its forepart is carved well and the pelvic and the tail fins are well brought out. Probably its dorsal fin is shown in appliqué with clay.

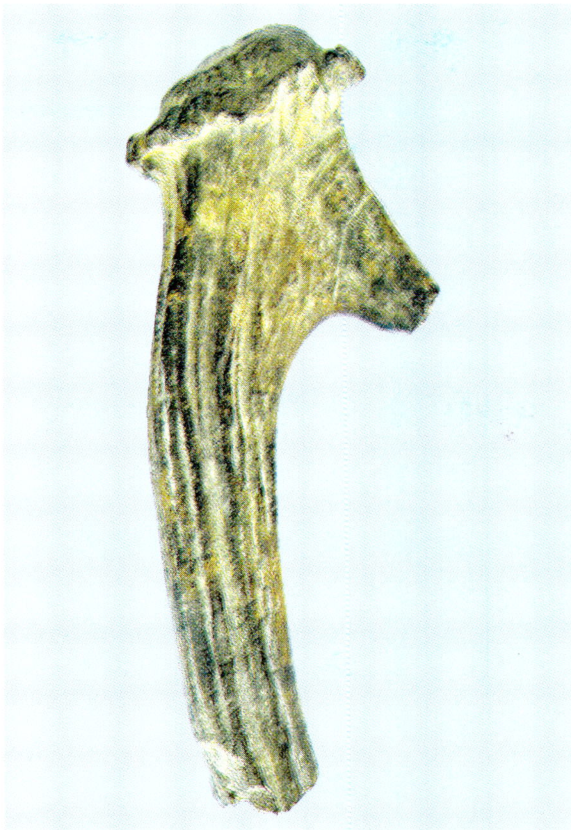

98. The antler (9 x 3.4 cm), depicts the face of an animal. Here, the artist takes opportunity of the peculiar formation of the antler itself in portraying the face. A shallow curved incised line and a short indentation summarily outline the face and the eye on the smaller branch, whereas the larger branch stands for the body. It is no wonder, if the artist depicted the face of a deer after it had been killed. If so, here we have certainly an instance conveying a compromise between a sense for the aesthetics and the faith reposed in the magi co-religious beliefs lending vitality to the enigmatic way of life of ancient man or else it was an instance of sympathetic magic.

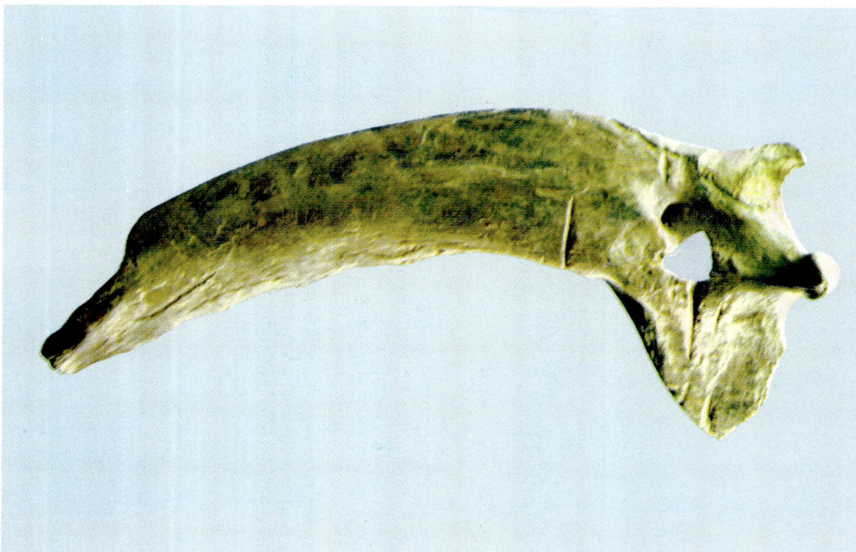

99. It is a lower jaw (L-9.7 cm), of some animal. Here the artist takes the opportunity of the peculiar formation of the bone and with the help of the engravings gives it the look of the face of an animal in profile.

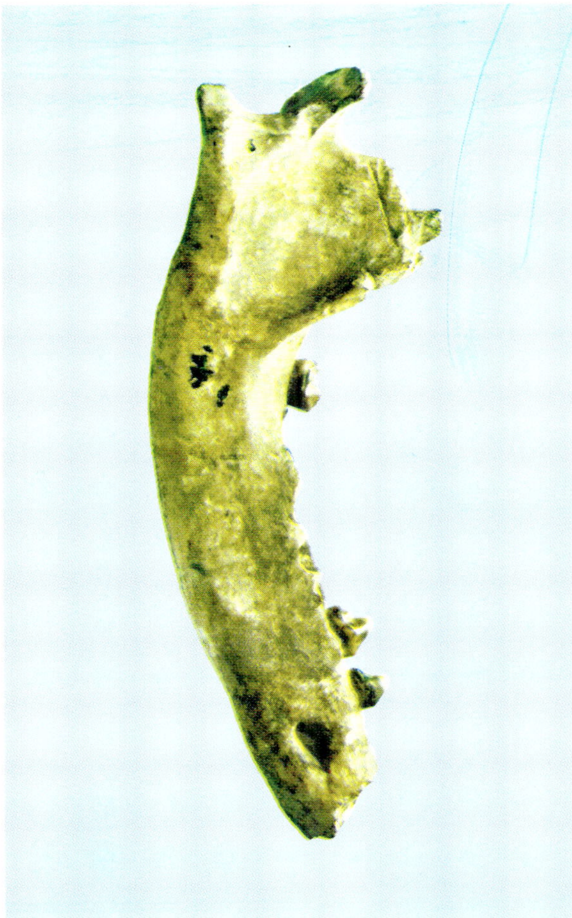

100. This jaw (L-11 cm), appears to be that of some carnivore. Engravings turn the upper portion to the form of some animal head. Traces of black painting are noticeable.

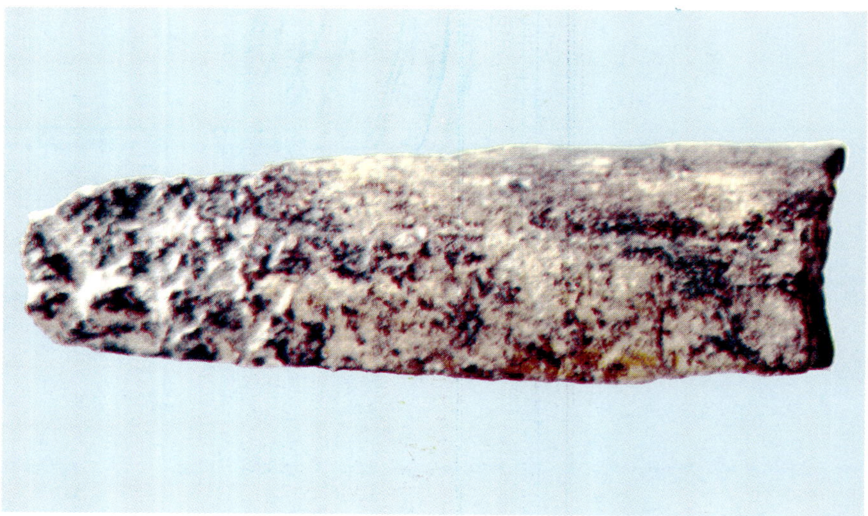

101. An animal in profile to left. The mouth is carved and engraved on the left border. Traces of black paint are noticeable. The specimen measures 6.5 x 2 cm.

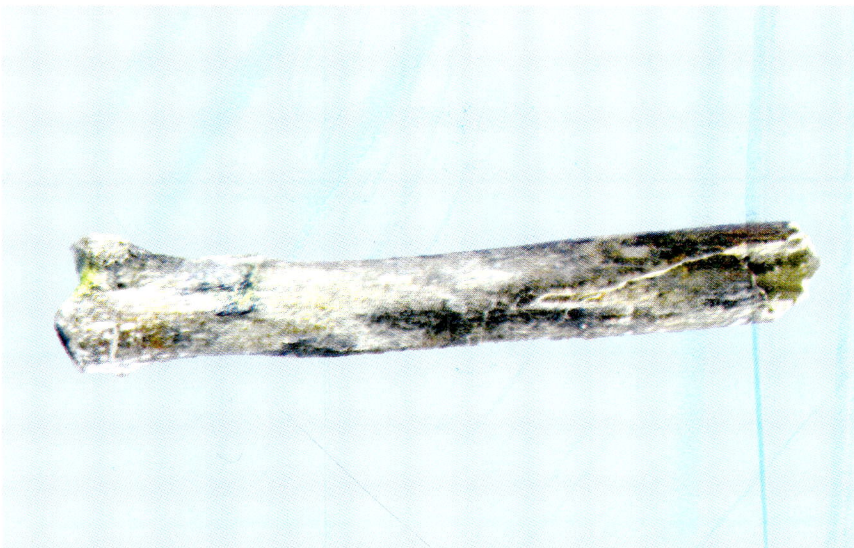

102. It is a slender cylindrical piece of bone (L-8.5 cm), black in colour. The natural curvature with engraved lines at right angle on left denoting mouth and a vertical engraved line a little away from the left border above denoting neck make sense of some beast to left.

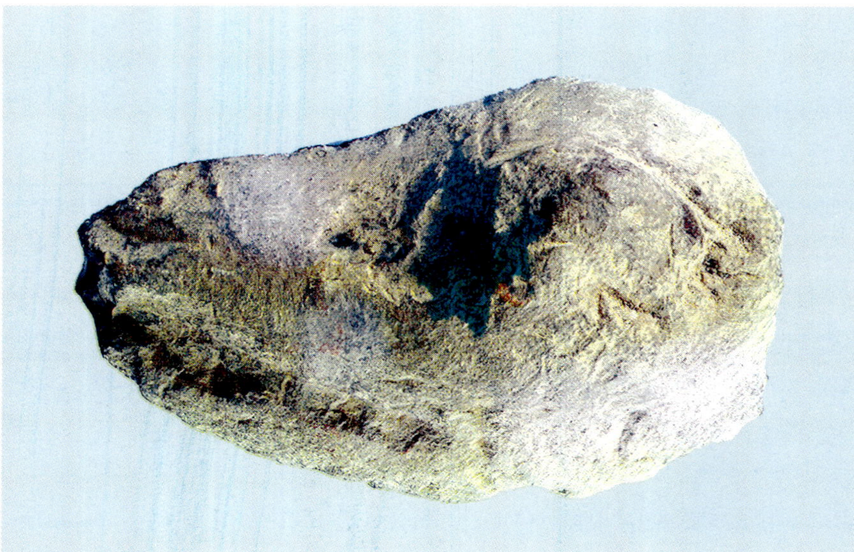

103. The specimen (10 x 7 cm), depicts an animal head in profile engraved on one half of a stone nodule. This is the only example of this kind collected from Natshal. It has been excluded from the table.

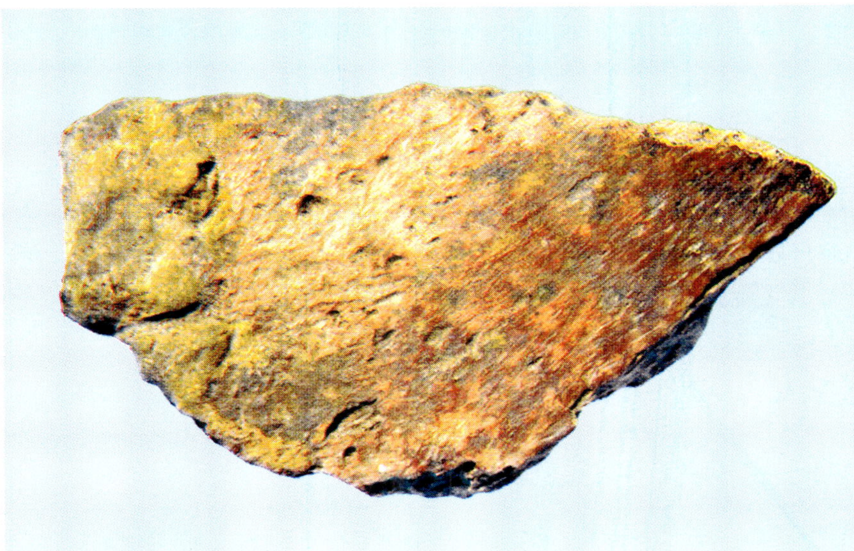

104. Semicircular or fan-shaped segment of bone (5 x 2.8 cm), probably represents a bird. A little of clay has been used to model the nose, mouth and the eye on left.

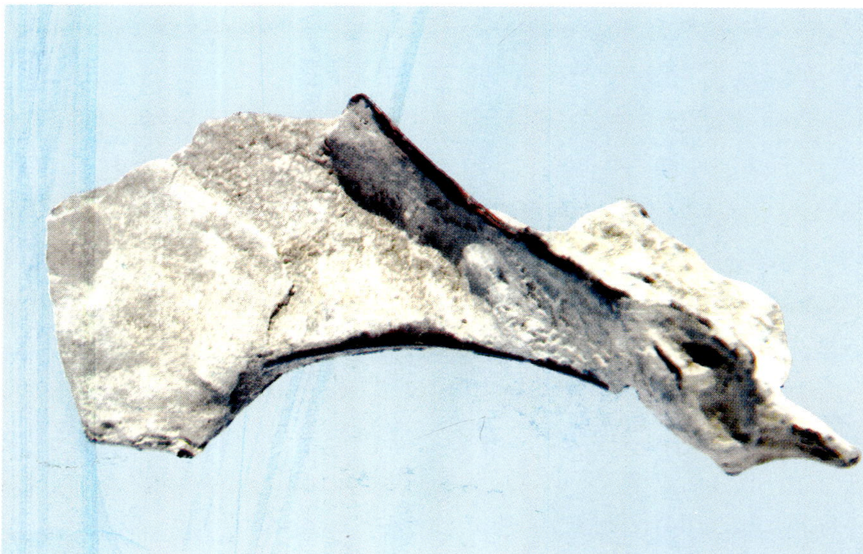

105. A segment of bone (5 x 2.2 cm), presenting an animal head to left in clay. The bone concerned was first besmeared with a polish of sticky white clay. Following it on the left extremity of the curved bone the head in profile has been modelled in clay. One eye, nostril and the mouth are well marked and the flesh well delineated.

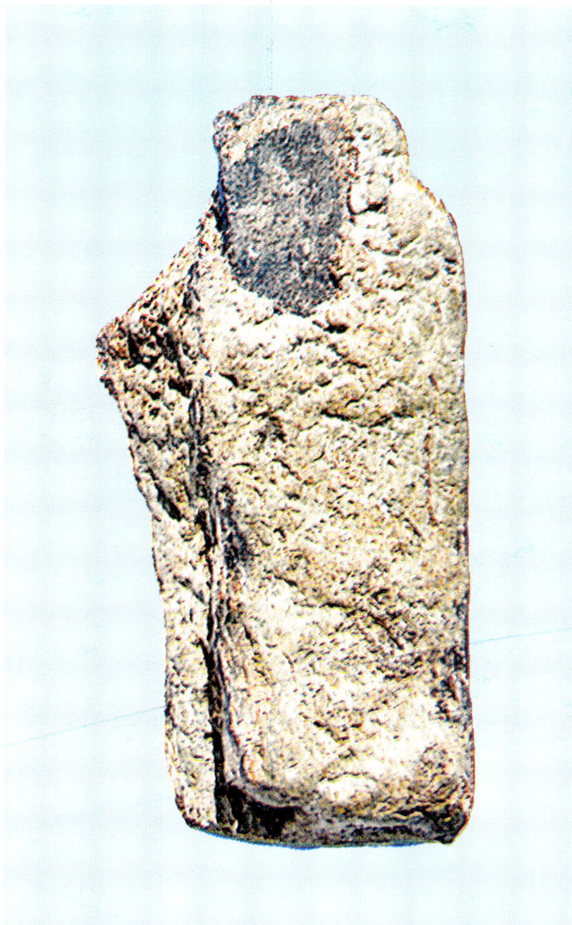

106. Human figures modelled in clay on a segment of bone (4.3 x 2.2 cm). The clay appears to be sun-baked. However, the massive and taller figure on right kisses the other on left. Though the heads are depicted in details, their bodies below neck are crudely represented in clay. It may represent coitus.

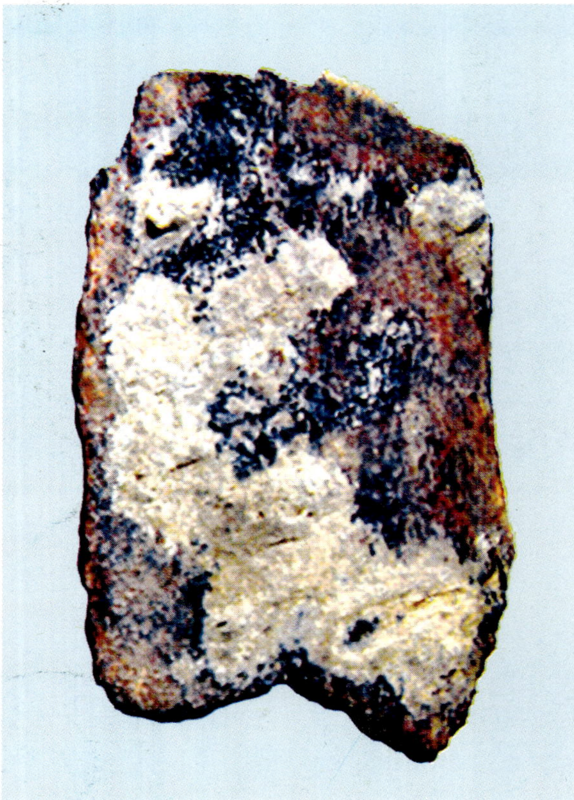

107. This almost a rectangular piece of bone (4.7 x 2.9 cm), was first painted in black and over it a human head in profile to left was modelled with a broad line of white clay with its open mouth, nose, forehead and cranium. Here the open mouth is presented frontally and the nose, forehead and cranium are depicted in profile.

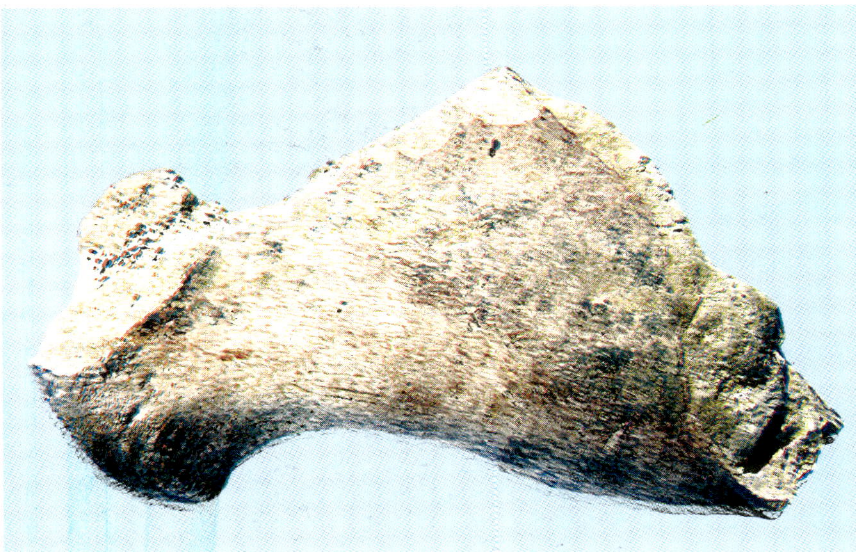

108. The flat piece of bone (7.2 x 3.3 cm), in the shape of an animal head to right. Though the lower and the left edges are retained intact, the upper and the right borders are achieved probably by cutting. While the right cheek is represented by the bone itself, the forehead, nose and the mouth are brought out by applying sticky white clay covering the border on right.

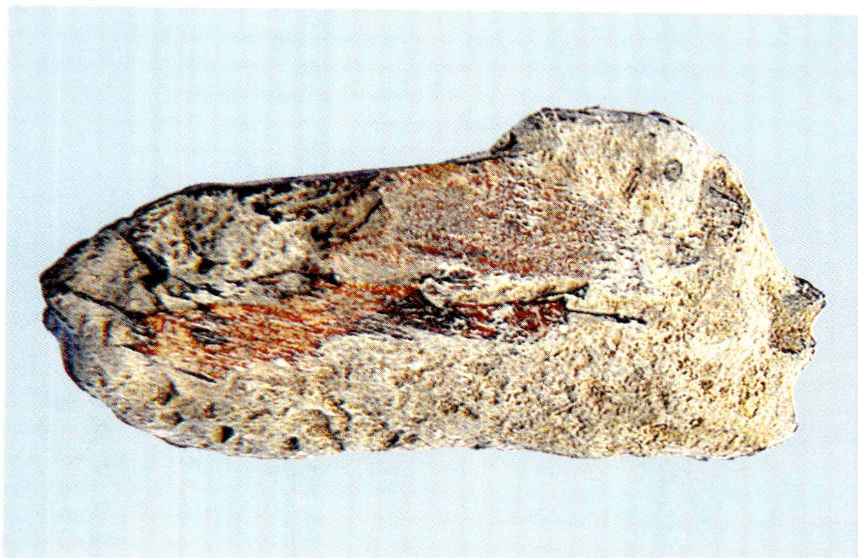

109. Segment of bone (4.1 x 2 cm), depicts on its right a human head in profile with clay. Sticky white clay is found along the border of the specimen. The bone was a scraper, probably.

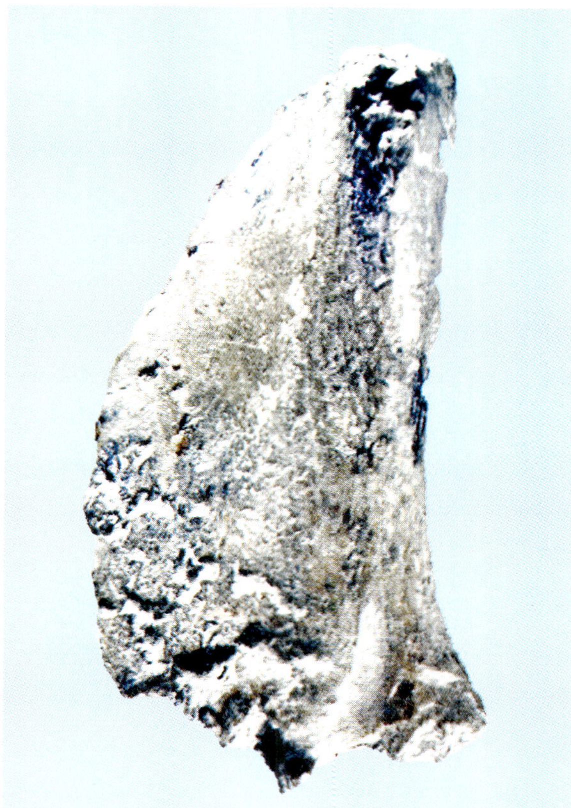

110 a). The specimen (4.6 x 2.5 cm), depicts two motifs on two sides – on one a human head and on another an animal head. On the present side, the human head with receding forehead is depicted in profile to left. The eye, small nose, mouth and the flesh on cheek are well marked and delineated by curved engravings.

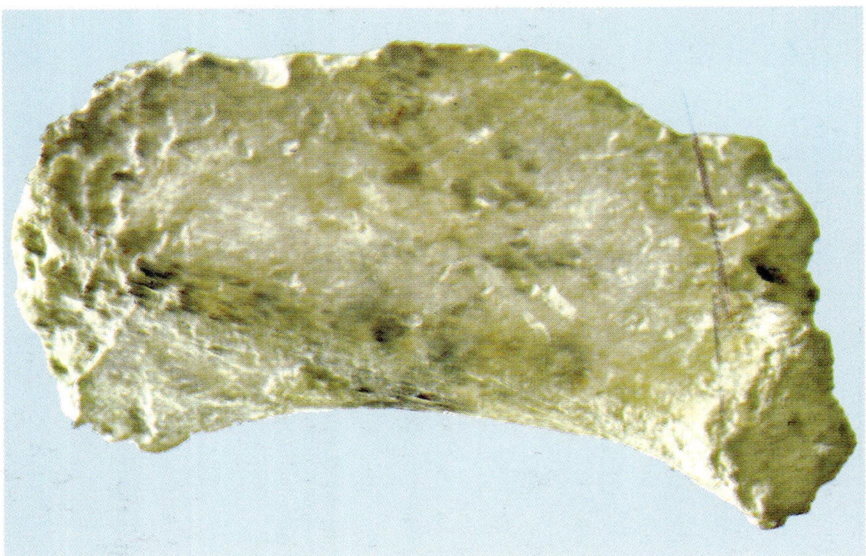

110 b). This side of the specimen depicts an animal head in profile to left. The mouth, the round and bulging eye and the hair on head and neck are well marked. These are engraved and pecked.

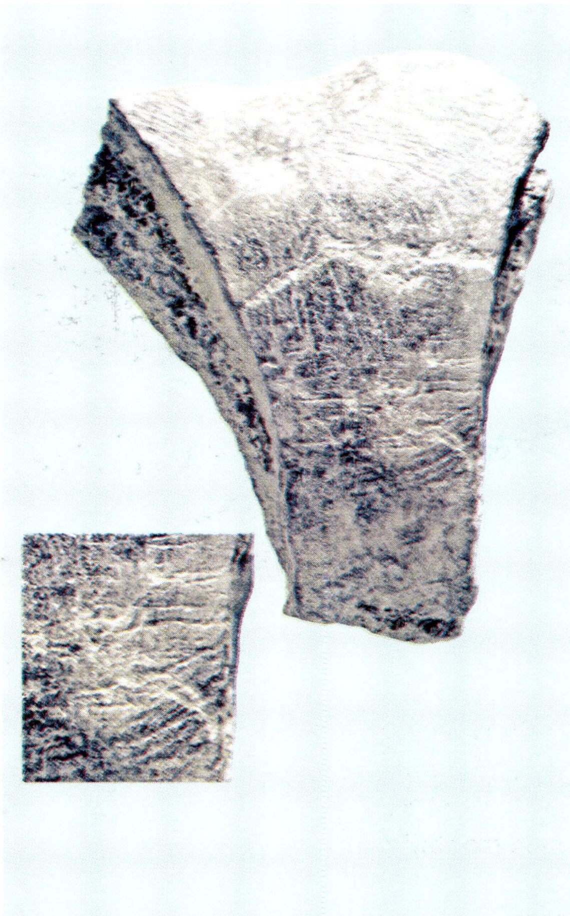

111 a) . The specimen (4.4 x 3.8 cm), is almost triangular and thick. On the present side, the forepart of the head of a wolf-like animal in profile to left is depicted. It is too small (.7 x .6 cm), and is likely to escape the notice of a casual observer.

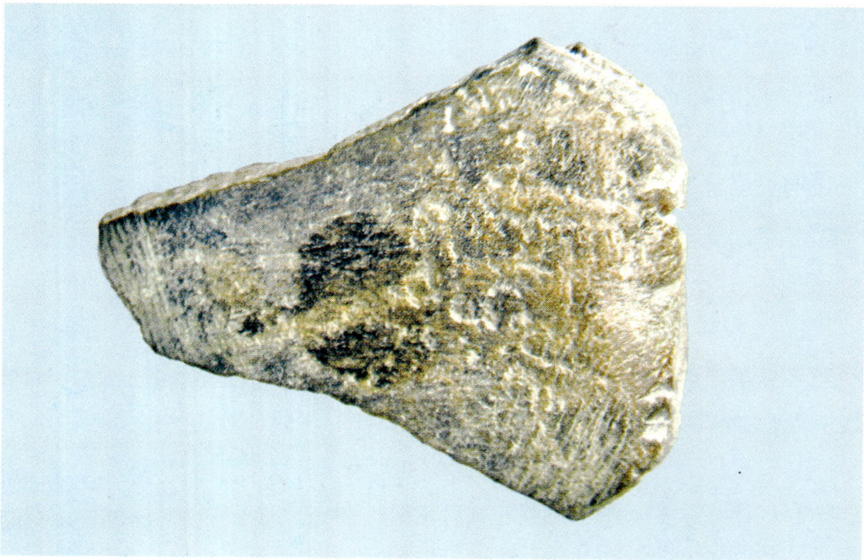

111 b). This side gives the side-view of a human head along the right border – the mouth below and the eye above. On the flat middle portion the lines of pin-holes probably give the outline of a human face frontally.

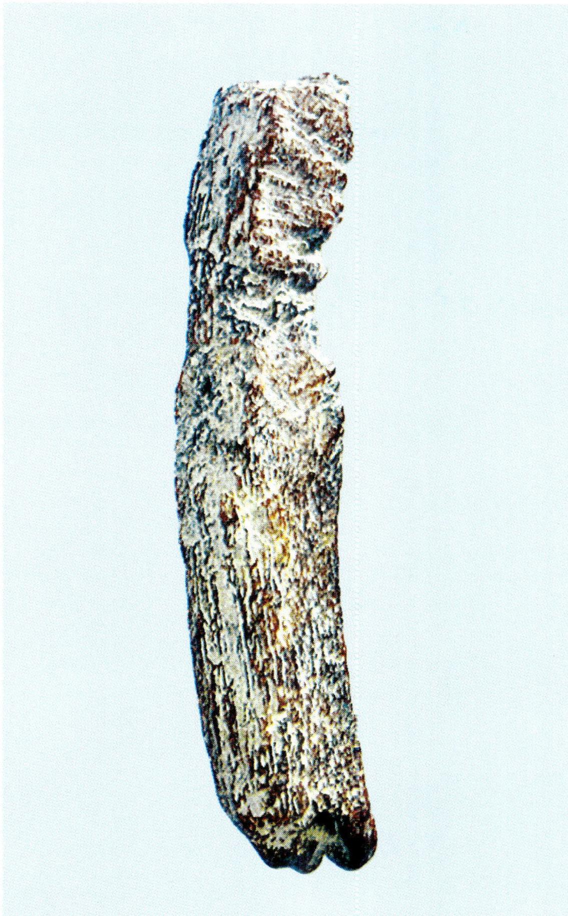

112 a). The side-view of a human face brought out by horizontal engraved lines. The portion below suggests the body. The specimen (5.7 x 1.2 cm), also depicts other motifs on its cross section.

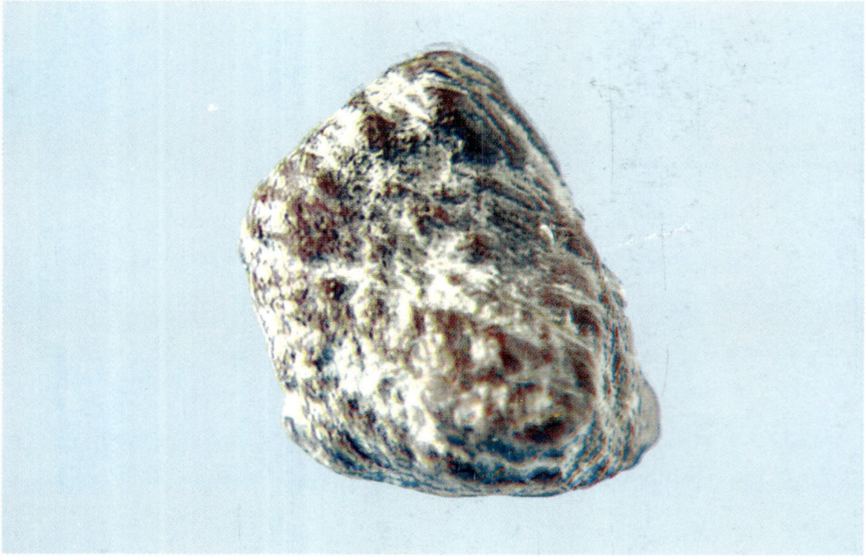

112 b). An animal face with bulging round eyes in relief and a wide open mouth is shown frontally. Another small face sharing the mouth in common is depicted below.

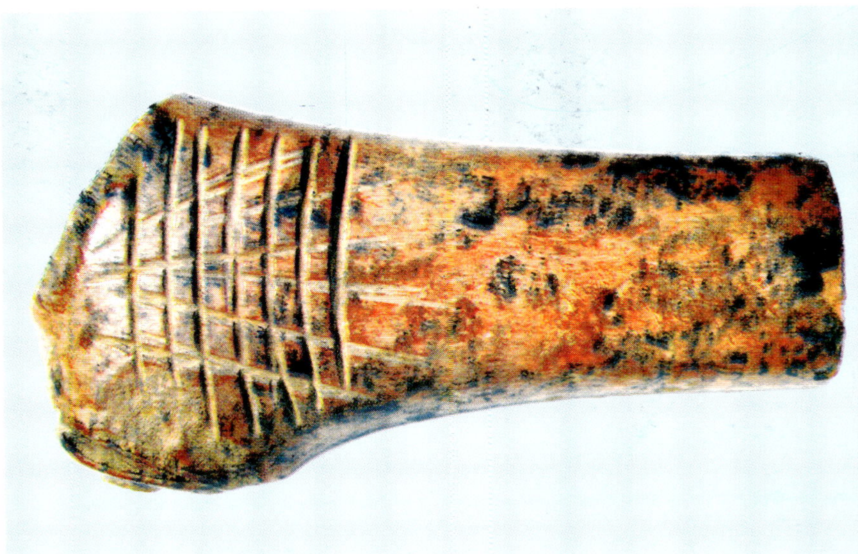

113 a). It is a piece of antler (L-7.8 cm). It is smooth and engraved with net design. Traces of black paint are noticeable on it.

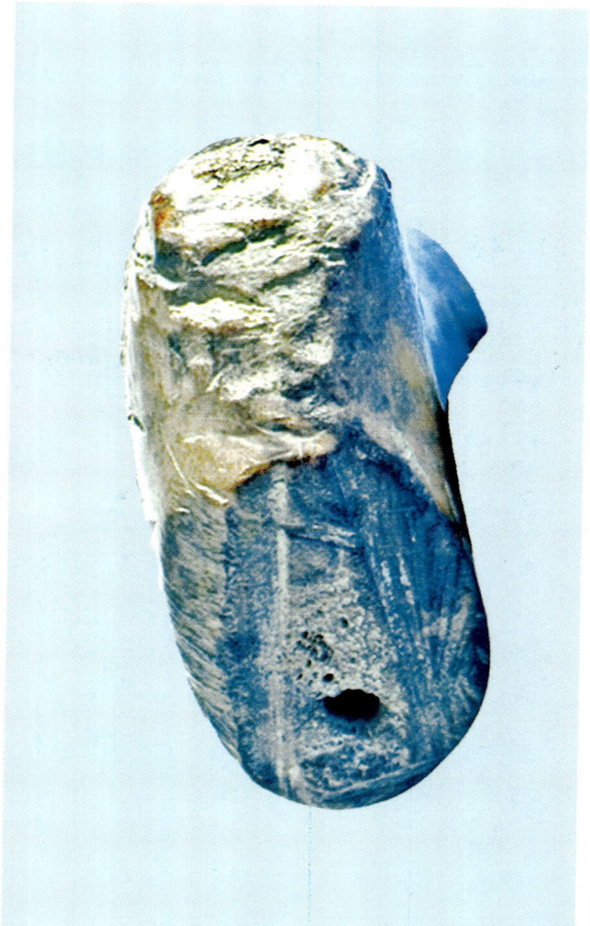

113 b). In the space between two branches of the antler that are cut and separated, a human face is depicted. Two round eyes are made by scooping out bits of material and the mouth is indicated by engraving.

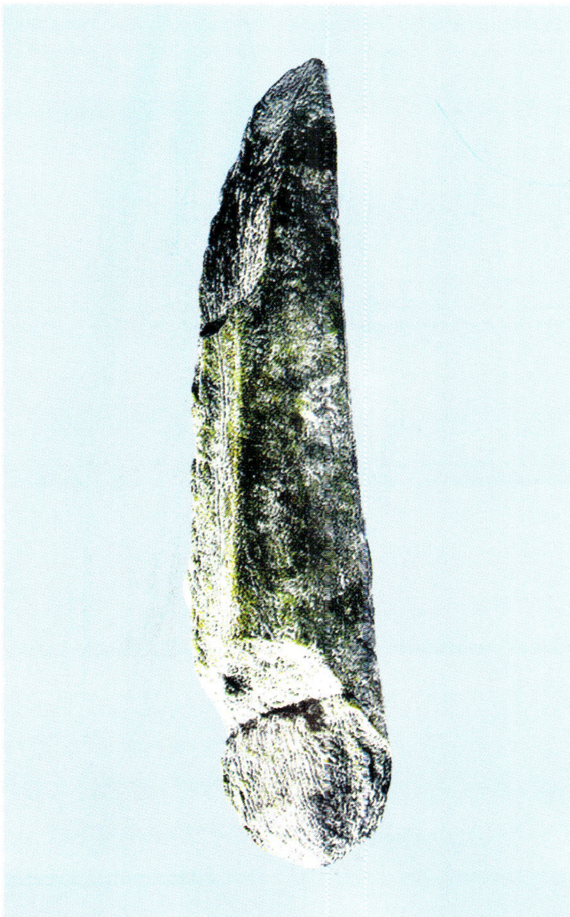

114. This specimen (5.8 x 1.2 cm), represents a phallus, circumcised realistically. The hole is shown probably to indicate the duct for passing of semen. It might have had some significance of fertility cult.

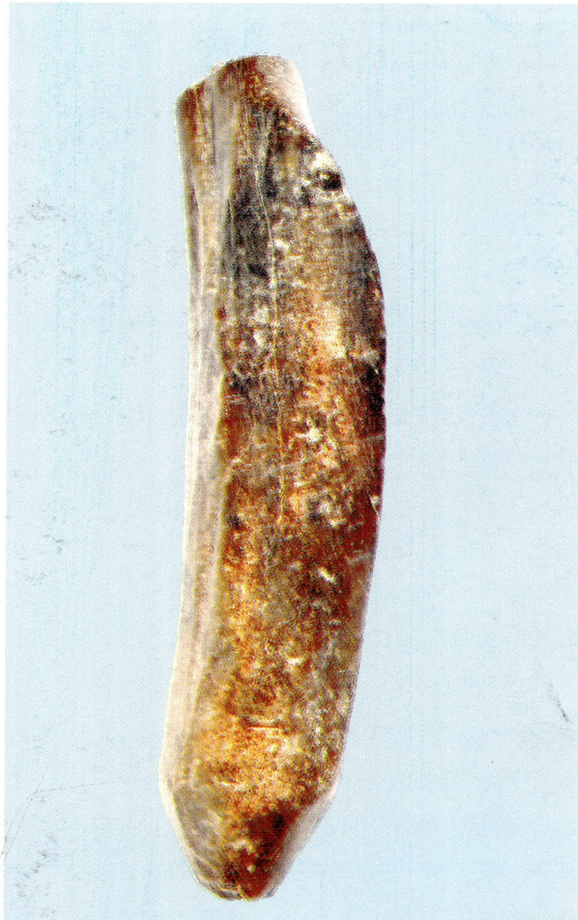

115. The antler (8 x 2.4 cm), portrays the features of both the vulva and the phallus combined. While the vulva is carved on the surface with a pin-hole in the middle, the phallus is carved at the narrow end with pin holes.

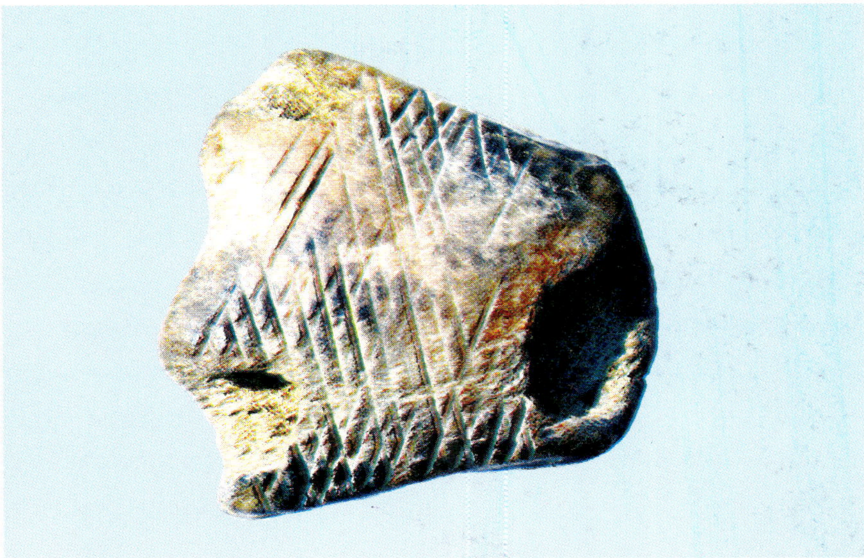

116. The specimen (4.5 x 4.5 cm), is a bead made of antler. It is painted in black and decorated with engraved net design. It has a horizontal hole to let the rope pass through.

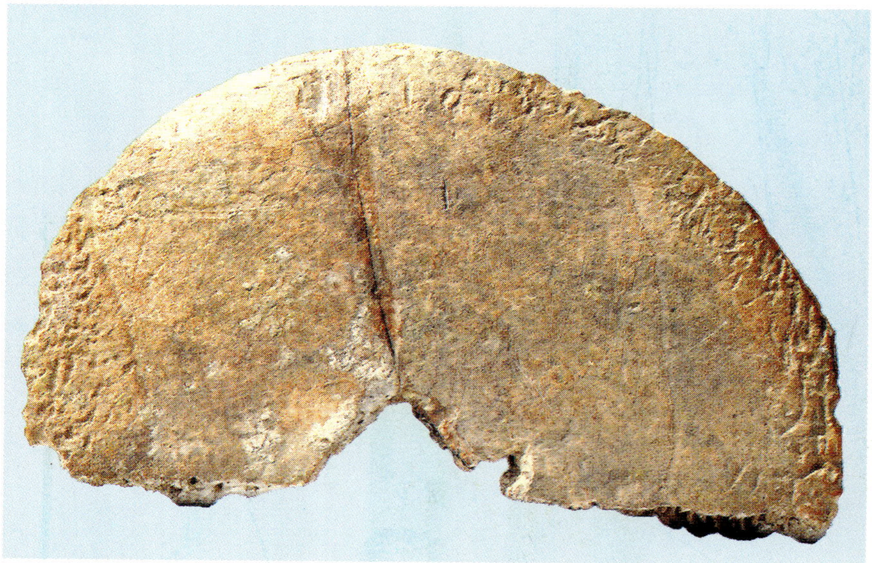

117. The specimen (19.3 x 5.6 cm), bears enigmatic engravings along its boarder on the dorsal side. As the concerned example does not betray any clear motif, it is excluded from the table. The border is shown in two segments in plates 117a and 117b depicting the enlarged engravings. The scholars doing research in the early art of writing may be benefited.

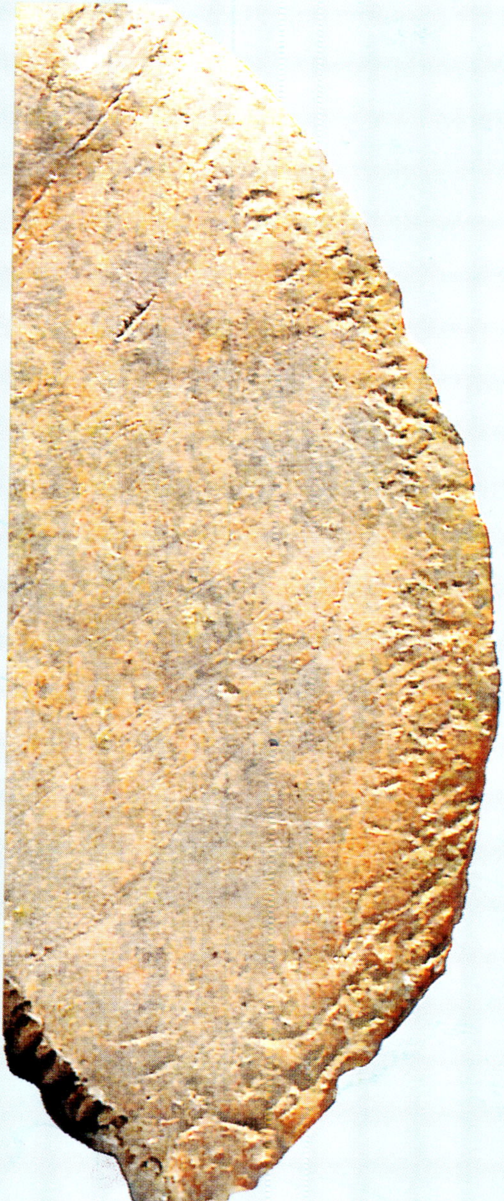

117a.

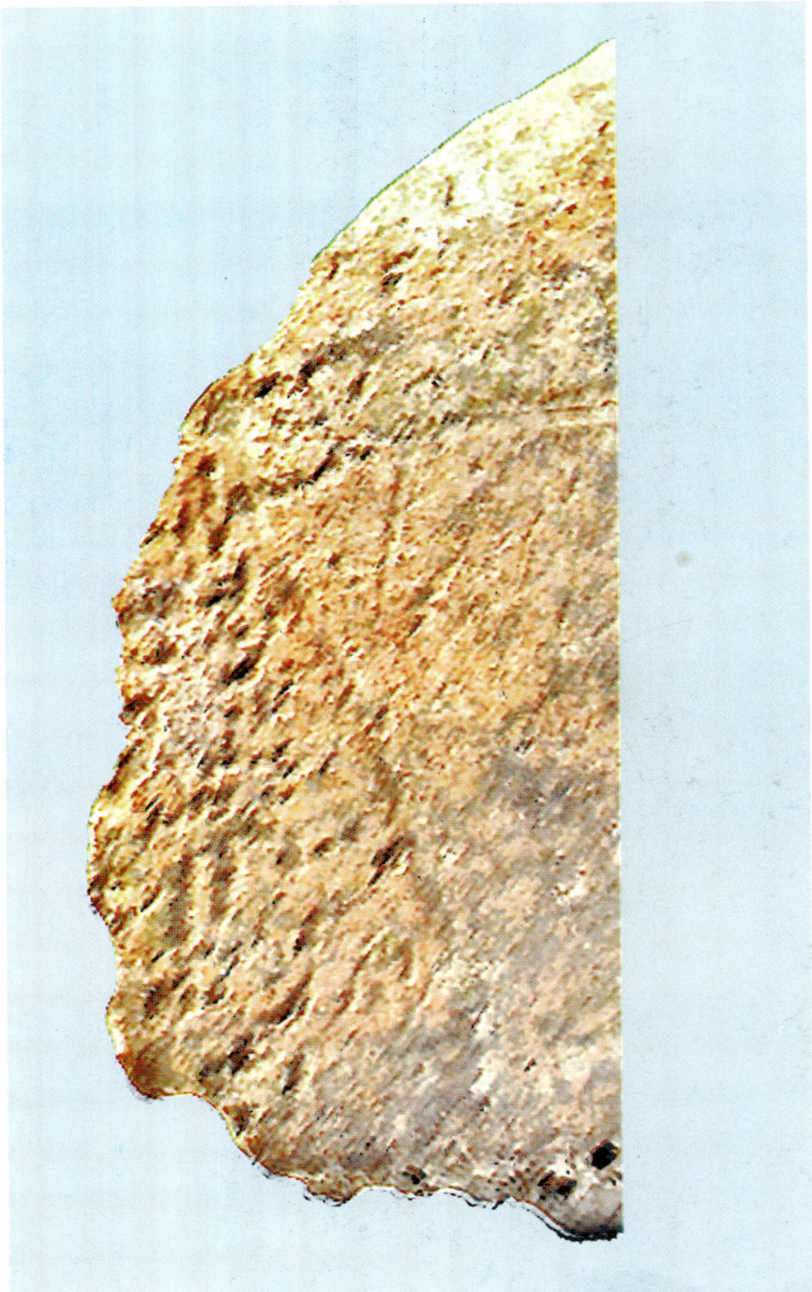

117b.